The Pressures of the Text

Orality, Texts and the Telling of Tales

Edited by
Stewart Brown

Birmingham University African Studies Series No.4
Centre of West African Studies
1995

ISBN 0-7044-1557-7

Printed in Great Britain by BPC Wheatons Ltd, Exeter

"The text only lives through the human voice"

Femi Oyebode

CONTENTS

INTRODUCTION

'The pressures of the text; orality, texts and the telling of tales'; it's an allusive and resonant title and the contributors to this volume come at it in a variety of ways, reflecting their different disciplinary backgrounds and their particular research interests at the time that the conference to which the drafts of these finished essays were presented[1] was held in May 1993. The theme was intentionally open. We were aware that several of the members of the Centre of West African Studies - staff, visiting fellows, graduate students - were working individually on areas and aspects of, for want of a better term, 'word culture' - in both Africa and the Caribbean - that were somehow between the traditional categories of oral and scribal literature, or were indeed engaged in challenging the validity of such categories and deconstructing the ideologies implicit in them. We decided, then, to use the annual round-table conference as a forum where such works-in-progress - both by members of CWAS and invited scholars working broadly in this field - would meet and their connections and contradictions would appear.

In the event several very fruitful areas of comparison emerged - across disciplines and across geographical areas. The ambiguity of the conference title - the pressures of the text - punning of course on Barthes' ironic subversion of the notion of "the pleasures of the text", but also echoing the West Indian critic Gordon Rohlehr's observation that even the most literary of writers must respond to the "pressures of orality" when he lives in a cosmopolitan, multicultural society like Trinidad - invites various responses. Is the text applying pressure or is it rather the victim of it? Is the pressure on texts to do with the status of orality as represented as text, or on the definition of text which might be expanded to accommodate the scriptless occasion of oral performance, or is the pressure on the nature of an orthography that can transcend the absence of cultural and contextual signifiers in the traditional materials of text ... Or is the pressure rather in the widespread notion of an hierarchical or competitive relationship between written texts and oral performance in which text signifies modernity and orality 'tradition', or where education is understood in terms of mastery of certain texts and orality equated with illiteracy ... ? Are the pressures of the text political and sociological rather than literary, related to changes in gender roles or the incursion of new technologies like video or the word-processor ...? Or is the word-processor potentially the tool that will liberate the text from the conventional limitations and pressures of orthography? All these possibilities and more were touched on in either the presentations or in the discussions which they generated.

1

The final versions of these papers, as they are published here, suggest the ways in which those discussions have shaped the individual scholar's re-thinking of issues. Several of the contributors take the opportunity to re-formulate some fundamental questions; Karin Barber, for example, who has long been engaged in a critique of the methodologies applied to the understanding and evaluation of oral materials, argues here that traditional notions of the distinctions between orality and text can be irrelevant to the process of composition. She draws on her first hand involvement in the Oyin Adejobi Theatre Company's productions in 1983 and discusses the ambivalent attitude members of that company had to the idea of a fixed written text; she posits the notion of an "imagined script" which occupies a conceptual space somewhere between text and improvisation. Understood slightly differently the idea of an "imagined script" resonates in relation to Nana Wilson-Tagoe's assertion - in regard to the relationship between Saint Lucian 'folk' mythology and Derek Walcott's otherwise very literary plays - that in some performance contexts,

"text is subsumed into the communicative event, deconstructed and made part of other modes of perception and cognition."

In the process of such a performance, she argues, songs and rituals taken from that 'folk' domain function as oral "counter texts" playing against the grain of the fixed dramatic script. Such are the "pressures of orality" that Rohlehr identified.

That pressure, albeit expressed in a more direct manner, begins to explain the necessary responsiveness of the popular dramatists - discussed in Al Creighton's essay on theatre in Guyana - to comments and criticisms voiced by those who make up their plays' audience. Rooted in notions of realism and the replication of 'lived experience' - including a concern with the language of the life the plays would represent - this popular drama has arguably created an audience for theatre in Guyana where one did not exist before. Creighton's essay explores the tension between that apparently narrow arena of popularly validated - and so almost co-voiced - drama and the ambitions of actors, playwrights and impresarios who would explore a more literary theatre.

That phrase "a more literary theatre" seems to imply that such a theatre must employ a different language than that which the audience for the popular plays Creighton describes would recognise as their own. The effect that an African writer's choice of an indigenous language for his work has in terms of its impact on an audience previously excluded by his use of English is examined in Kabir Ahmed's essay on Ngugi wa Thiong'o's novel *Devil on the Cross*. He examines the extent to which Ngugi is forced to borrow from and adapt the techniques of orality in the construction of a text which will actually work for an audience not at all used to the manners and conventions of the European novel. Beyond the 'simple' adoption of another language Ngugi has to employ an appropriately idiomatic usage which is both capable of sustaining the narrative thrust of his long novel and of holding his newly won audience. In their essay Carolyn Cooper and Hubert Devonish argue that in the Caribbean context too, the debate around the status of the languages West Indian people actually speak is much more serious a matter than the tone of much of the literary in-fighting might suggest, rather that the "contest ... between a literature and an orature" is a matter of national and political identity. The Bajan cultural establishment's resistance to the kind of popular materials that Curwen Best examines in his essay is perhaps an example of the ground over which that battle for cultural identity is being fought. Best pays close attention to the social dynamics that inform the production and reception of popular song in Barbados, highlighting the many instances of what he calls "interactive cross-over" - between genres, between art-forms and between linguistic registers. Echoing Gordon Rohlehr's demand for "a different notion of crafting" in relation to forms of West Indian word culture that don't fit comfortably into any of the existing literary categories, Best laments the absence of a shared critical vocabulary or of a methodology that will do justice to the particular qualities of the performances he is concerned with. Philip Nanton's essay takes this argument further by questioning the validity of some of the assumptions that those critics sympathetic to the oral dimension of Caribbean word culture have made and is particularly critical of the way the notion of a "linguistic continuum" has fudged what he sees as important boundaries between orality and textuality.

Those issues around the cultural assumptions critics make, which must bear on both their sensitivity and their competence, are also raised by both Femi Oyebode and Ato Quayson in their essays here. Both are concerned with the relationship between literary texts by contemporary Nigerian authors and the oral traditions which to some extent inform and shape them. A fine poet himself - as we discovered by his reading during the conference - Oyebode is particularly interested in the characteristic qualities of oral poetries in terms of the range of rhetorical and prosodic devices which are employed in different forms of - particularly Yorùbá - oral poetry. Some contemporary Yorùbá poets, he argues, although writing in English, have been very much aware of those prosodic devices which to some extent form their understanding of what poetry *is*. Several of those poets, he suggests, have attempted to adapt and apply those techniques and devices to the poetry they write in English. Few critics, particularly European and American critics, he argues, are even aware that such tensions are being exploited by these writers. Consequently they fail to recognise the effects the poets strive for and sometimes make negative judgements about lack of 'craft' or 'music' in such poetry when in fact the shape of the poems on the page has been largely determined by a different understanding of those terms. Ato Quayson asks fundamental questions about the theoretical assumptions critics have made about the relationship between African writers and the oral traditions their texts are so often said to relate to and draw on. Quayson is wary of the tendency for critics to

3

'homogenise' African cultures generally and - as Oyebode asserts - to ignore the specificity of particular oral traditions and styles. He goes on to examine the work of two writers who have to some extent been victims of this critical ignorance - Amos Tutuola and Ben Okri - and offers very closely contextualised readings of ways those writers have adapted the devices and effects of particular Yorùbá oral narratives.

Ada Adeghe's essay makes a similar point with regard to the necessity for critics of African literatures to be better informed, culturally, before they make negative judgements about a writer's work. Adeghe's particular focus is on the relationship between 'traditional' notions of gender roles, including specific forms of orature reserved for women in certain cultures, and the characteristics of fiction written in English by Nigerian women authors. The challenge to literary critics that such complex social and cultural nuances as Oyebode, Quayson and Adeghe point up is as nothing, really, compared to the challenge actually faced by the writers in trying to find/make a language on-the-page which will be capable of *expressing* those cultural and often essentially oral forms, echoes and nuances. One writer who has foregrounded that struggle - which is perhaps particularly intense because so much of his work is located in the cultural cross-over between West Africa and the Caribbean - has been Kamau Brathwaite. Stewart Brown's paper here examines the orthographic and textual strategies Brathwaite has employed throughout his career but looks particularly at the 'Sycorax video style' he has developed in very recent works, employing the graphic and typographical capacities of the word-processor to, in his words, "write in light" that "consciousness of ourselves" which traditional texts could not accommodate.

Brathwaite's Sycorax video texts, then, are in one sense "imagined scripts" - which returns us (perhaps too neatly!) to Karin Barber's paper which opens the volume. But the connections are there and the value of this collection of essays - beyond the quality and interest of individual contributions - is in the surprise of finding such unexpected linkages between the tellings of such disparate tales.

Thanks are due to the many people who were involved in different ways in making both the conference and this volume happen. I should particularly like to thank Karin Barber for her enthusiasm, encouragement and support for the whole enterprise; Cathy Goodman, whose contribution to the organisation and smooth running of the conference was much appreciated by all who attended; and Isabelle James who has taken great trouble with the typing and preparation of what has sometimes proved - for the editor at least - a blood-pressure-raising text.

Stewart Brown

---

1   The exception is the essay by Carolyn Cooper and Hubert Devonish, which wasn't delivered at the conference because the writers were unable to travel from Jamaica to attend. Two papers which were given but which, for various

reasons, the authors have decided not to publish here, were presented by Kathy Williams (University of Warwick) and Fírinne Ní Chréacháin (CWAS). Other scholars attending the conference included Obi Maduakor (University of Calabar, Nigeria) and Cathy Olayinka Goodman (CWAS).

Literacy, Improvisation and the Public
in Yorùbá Popular Theatre*

Karin Barber

Aspiration to the condition of writing

In Africanist literary criticism, romanticism still surrounds the notion of 'orality'. Even in post-colonial critical discourses informed by a destabilising irony, 'orality' sometimes remains the last unexamined, essentialist concept, projected as an imagined antithesis of writing. It is a highly value-charged term, which can be accorded almost talismanic authority. The mode of orality, underlying and breaking through into written, Anglophone or Francophone texts, is what is said to give such texts their distinctive Africanity. Eileen Julien has brilliantly exposed its role, in much Francophone criticism, as guarantor of 'authenticity' (Julien 1992). It is treated as both a source - the origin and precursor of 'modern' literature - and a resource - a rich heritage or fund of themes, motifs, images, and techniques upon which the 'modern' author can draw. According to Abiola Irele, the 'distinctive mark' of written African literature in European languages is 'the striving to attain the condition of oral expression, even within the boundaries established by Western literary conventions' (Irele 1990:63).

Yorùbá popular itinerant theatre, however, displays exactly the opposite tendency. It is a form that in actual fact and practice appears predominantly oral, in the sense that the plays are improvised, unscripted, and collectively produced by the collaborative interaction of performers with each other and with audiences, drawing on repertoires of accumulated idioms and strategies of characterisation. But it aspires to the condition of writing, and is deeply internally configured by this aspiration. The presence of 'writing' as a point of orientation in this theatre - in its organisation, its preparation and in its actual performance - is much more than a polite bow in the direction of the better-educated. In my view it is a clue to the project of the theatre.

*I am deeply indebted to the friends and colleagues at Northwestern University who helped me to revise this paper during the year I spent at the Institute for Advanced Study and Research in the African Humanities. They include Keith Breckenridge, Catherine Burns, Catherine Cole, Stephan Miescher, Sandra Richards and Virginia Stewart. I also benefited greatly from the discussion of versions of it at seminars at Berkeley, Stanford, Madison-Wisconsin and Chicago universities. Thanks also to Paulo Farias for his invaluable suggestions.

Recently, a number of interventions in the theory of orality and literacy have dismantled the earlier model of a universal cognitive and cultural divide between the 'oral' and the 'literate'. Instead, they have offered accounts of specific, localised cultural configurations which show that reading and writing, like oral production and reception, take historically specific forms, and that almost everywhere, oral and written forms of discourse interpenetrate, sometimes antagonistically and sometimes in a mutually constitutive way (Boyarin 1993, Hofmeyr 1994, Street 1993). In this paper, I propose to show how the writing-saturated orality of the Yorùbá popular theatre offers clues to the constitution of a whole field of contemporary local popular culture.

Contemporary Yorùbá (and perhaps Nigerian and even African) popular culture has in the past been obscured by the dichotomising paradigms through which it has been viewed. A sentimentally valorised 'pure' orality (the voice, par excellence, of the Other) has been linked with 'tradition' (the pre-colonial past still existing in the present) and with the 'indigenous' (expressed in African languages). The oral, traditional, indigenous arts have been opposed to the written, modern, Europhone or exogenously-inspired ones. These dichotomies have been reflected in the distribution of scholarly studies of Yorùbá culture, which have overwhelmingly dealt *either* with such forms as masquerades, wood carving and Ifá divination, *or* with the modern, English-language writings of Ṣoyinka, Oṣọfisan et al. The huge field of contemporary popular Yorùbá culture - of which the itinerant theatre is a powerful example - falls between these two stools. To talk of it in terms of hybridity, simply marrying the two halves of the established dichotomies, as I have done in the past (Barber 1987), does not give much leverage on questions about the experience, purposes or consciousness of the participants in this culture. Literacy in colonial and post-colonial western Nigeria has been the centre of an ideological force-field of ideas about progress, self-improvement and modernity even for the many people who make little practical use of writing in their everyday lives. The actors in the popular theatre do not need writing to stage a play, but they choose to highlight the idea of the written text at every opportunity, as a mode of self-definition. It is their views that I wish to consider in this discussion.

This analysis would offer a point of entry, I believe, into a larger project to be undertaken in future: an attempt to characterise the nature of the 'public sphere' occupied and in part created by the new forms of popular communication and entertainment that exploded into life in western Nigeria in the colonial and post-colonial periods.

At present, however, the kind of cultural documentation needed to take on these questions has hardly been broached. Little has been written directly about the everyday perceptions and experiences of the broad, heterogeneous, fluctuating categories of Yorùbá people that, since the 1940s, have been the main producers and consumers of the new popular cultural forms.¹ These 'intermediate classes' - who are neither agrarian workers nor the highly visible elite - are most often described by lists of occupations: motor mechanics, drivers, tailors, petty traders, bricklayers, primary school teachers. They escape definition because they are both geographically and socially mobile. The service sector of the western Nigerian economy was massively swollen by the advent of cocoa wealth and then, in the 1970s and early 80s, by that of the petro-naira, which drew large numbers of people away from farming into trading and small-scale artisanal enterprises.² According to Fapohunda (1978) half the population of Lagos is engaged in 'informal sector' activities, and all western Nigerian cities have similar sectors, if not on the same scale. But, as Berry (1985) shows, each occupation (including farming itself) is seen as a means to accumulate funds in order to diversify into other enterprises. People are always moving on, in the hope of moving up. With a few exceptions, these entrepreneurs operate precariously and on a small scale. They belong, in general, to the poorer and less educated half of the population.

In the colonial period and after, it was these categories of people - mobile, entrepreneurial, and struggling to better themselves - who took the lead in creating new genres of popular expression to speak to new experience. Almost all these genres were directly or indirectly associated with school education, the church, and 'modernity'. All addressed larger, more anonymous and often more dispersed publics than older genres such as masquerade, festival drama, and oral poetry. Circulating between live performance, electronic media and print, themes and motifs gained wide dissemination in multiple forms. The popular theatre is a central site in these fields of mutating discourse, feeding on histories, novels, newspapers, street talk, oral anecdotes, sermons and tales for its sources, and supplying magazines, television, records, radio, films and video with materials to recirculate. The audiences that crowd to see them tend to be conversant with all of these discourses, and even supply suggestions and materials for their elaboration.

Yorùbá popular theatre

Yorùbá popular theatre became a well-established form in the 1940s and 50s. Its starting point was in the church, where choirmasters and choirs collaborated to produce 'Bible operas': sung dramas on Biblical themes, performed in the church itself and designed to attract converts and raise funds to build more churches. However, from the very beginning another cultural strand deriving from popular music and imported vaudeville shows was entwined with the Biblical materials, and very quickly, groups of performers responded to a voracious audience demand for entertainment by moving into secular, folkloric or contemporary themes and into secular performance venues such as town halls, hotels and schools (Jeyifo

1984). By the 1970s many of these groups were becoming fully professional, commercial, touring theatres. By 1980 there were estimated to be over a hundred of them. The most popular of them played to large audiences wherever they went, at times filling entire football stadia. In the mid-1980s, economic catastrophe and a growing preference for film began to undermine the live theatre, and by the early 1990s most of the theatre companies had more or less stopped performing on stage. Some closed down; the more successful or fortunate ones put their efforts into making films, video dramas and television shows. The performances and conversations discussed here date from the high point of the theatre, in the 1980s.

In its self-presentation this theatre was consciously modern, deliberately distinguishing itself from older forms of drama such as *egúngún* and *gèlèdé* masquerade shows by its use of space and equipment. The popular theatre always played on platform stages before an audience seated on chairs in rows. They always used stage scenery (usually a backcloth, two or three sets of flats, and a curtain), electric lighting (usually a combination of spot lights and bundles of fluorescent strip lights, laid horizontally along the front of the stage) and a system of amplifiers and microphones, around which the actors choreographed their exchanges and projected them to the noisy audiences. In their espousal of modernity, they reproduced the performance spaces of church and school. Newer developments in Western theatre - theatre in the round, mobile multi-space performances - were out of the question, for they represent the West's attempt to reclaim theatrical uses of space which the masquerade theatres of Nigeria had never lost. Similarly, the Yorùbá theatre companies clung to a rather old-fashioned Western dramatic form - the temporally linear narrative drama with well-defined sequences of action, realistically-presented characters, and formal coherence and closure - for these distinguished them from the aggregative, segmented style of the older theatrical forms in Nigeria.

But in its techniques of rehearsal, in the creation and performance of a play, the popular theatre groups did not use the 'modern' Western method of producing a play from a written script. One or two theatre leaders published versions of plays they had performed, as another outlet and a further source of revenue; but these texts existed in parallel with the performed play, rather than being antecedent to it. Nor can the theatre of the 1980s be seen as a transitional stage in a progression from 'traditional' orality to 'modern' literacy, for if anything, the improvisatory character of the production process intensified over the years. The early 'Bible Operas' were almost entirely sung. The words of the songs were often written down to aid memorisation by the cast. Several such texts of Hubert Ogunde's early 1940s plays exist. It is significant that when passages of spoken dialogue occurred, these were merely indicated in the text with a stage direction: it was not thought necessary to write them out. Over the years, the songs in all theatre companies' plays were gradually reduced and the amount of spoken dialogue increased. This was partly a result of the influence of television, in which a number of theatre companies became involved almost from its inception in the Western Region in 1959. Television producers demanded a more naturalistic style of presentation, which in due course affected the live stage plays as well. The plays became more improvisatory, and the use of a written song-text was dropped. By the 1980s, most theatre companies had substantial repertoires of plays, all unscripted, which they could keep in existence for many years through the exercise of collective memory and re-creation.

Education and the 'intermediate classes'

The people of western Nigeria manifested, from the beginning of the century, a voracious desire for schooling. As early as 1912, more than twice as many pupils were being taught in schools unassisted by the government - many of them 'private venture schools' rather than mission schools, 'conducted for profit by half-educated youths' - than were attending government and government-assisted schools (Fafunwa 1974:112). Elementary education equipped these pupils to become 'a clerk, a teacher, a catechist or a letter-writer' (ibid.). The colonial authorities attempted to restrain this expansion, arguing that employment opportunities were limited and a plethora of 'educated natives' running round causing trouble was undesirable. The demand was so strong, however, that the colonial government compromised by widening access to a six-year primary course but providing few places at secondary level. This trend was greatly reinforced by the programme of the Action Group, which came to office in the Western Region in 1952 largely on the strength of its promise of Universal Primary Education - a promise which was fulfilled, to all intents and purposes, as early as 1960, when 90% of children of school age were enrolled. By the time I attached myself to the theatre company in 1981, then, a huge category of Primary 6 leavers had been created. They left school more or less literate in English and Yorùbá, conversant with English dates, times, and counting systems, and also familiar with some of the large body of Yorùbá-language written literature that had been produced since the 1940s.

Much of the popular theatre's audience, and many of its actors, belonged to this category of school-leavers. In the Oyin Adéjọbí Theatre Company in 1983, two members had been to Primary School but dropped out in Year 5. Another five had completed primary school. Five had gone on to Modern School, a three-year post-primary course intended as preparatory to Teacher Training. Only one - Adéjọbí's own daughter, who was only a part-time performer - had been to Grammar School and taken her WAEC (equivalent to O-level) exams. But none of them had missed going to school altogether. In general, then, it could be said that they had had some schooling, but did not belong to the educated élite. The jobs that many of them trained for after primary school, before they joined the theatre, were typical of the informal sector as described by Fapohunda (1978) and Berry (1985). They included welding, truck- and taxi-driving, mechanic, 'rewire', 'radionic', 'tailoring' (done by men), 'sewing' (done by women), 'ward-maid' in a private maternity hospital, clerk to a trader, and petty trading.

The theatre was implicated in the world of schooling, which was definitive of the actors' view of themselves and of society. Many of them had entered the theatre as a profession because of a liking for drama formed at school. Most Primary Schools put on 'end-of-year' plays. They were also visited by itinerant professional companies who performed in the school hall at cut rates. John Adéwuni, one of the leading actors in the Oyin Adéjọbí Theatre Company, described his participation like this:

> What encouraged me [to become an actor] was that, when I was at school, anything to do with singing, acting, I was very interested in it. Drumming, I was very interested in it. If a theatre group came to perform for us, I would be the first person to go and find out what it was they'd come to do. And if we were doing an end-of-year play, as we used to do in Primary School, I would be at the drums, I would drum. I would be the person to play the biggest role in all the school plays, and from that time on I decided that if I didn't work as a singer, I would work as an actor. [My translation.]

As actors, they continued to maintain the link between schools and theatre by their frequent performances to boarding-school audiences.

The cultural world associated with Primary School leavers is constituted, in part, by novels and plays published in Yorùbá; by neo-traditional poetry which is rendered, simultaneously, as published texts and oral performances disseminated via radio, television, and records as well as live events; and by magazines, including the fortnightly *Atọka*, a 'photoplay' magazine which represents actual popular stage plays by means of sequences of staged photographs, with bubble captions added. The pages of *Atọka* include many letters from young people asking for pen-pals and consulting the Agony Auntie; and they, like the theatre company members, describe themselves as welders, drivers, tailors, and clerks, as well as school pupils.

One of the Adéjọbí Company's actors, Sunday Fágbáyìímú, gives a wonderful insight into some of the elements that go into the constitution of this public's consciousness. Sunday could not continue his education after Primary School because his parents did not have the means (he blames this on the fact that his father was polygamous). He was sent from his parents' 'village' to Ìbàdàn to learn trading from his elder brother, and after two years' apprenticeship set up on his

11

own, hawking 'fancy' (haberdashery and underwear) in the 'go-slow' (lines of immobilised traffic in the semi-permanent urban jam). At the same time he was determined to further his education by himself. He attended night school and took correspondence courses, and achieved considerable fluency in English. (He insisted that I interview him in English, even though he habitually spoke Yorùbá - as did all the theatre company members - in his daily life.) After some years of success in his trade, he suffered 'breakdown', and had to return to his parents' village. While there, he studied *ewì*, a form of neo-traditional poetry which offers moral reflections and political comment on modern life, in idioms drawn from the older repertoires of *oríkì* and Ifá. His goal was to have an '*ewì* business': that is, to become a professional writer and performer of *ewì* like Lánrewájú Adépòjù and Túnbòsun Oládàpò, who make their living from their performances and their published volumes of poetry. He had seen and heard these great '*ewì* exponents' perform on radio and television; but he stressed that he had taught himself *ewì* mainly by reading and studying the published texts. He began to write *ewì* himself, and perform them at important celebrations in the village. On his return to Ìbàdàn, he apprenticed himself to Lánrewájú Adépòjù, and since Adépòjù also ran a theatre group (and published a play which this theatre group had created[3]), he gained experience of acting which stood him in good stead when he applied to join the Adéjobí Theatre. He told me that his greatest ambitions were, first, to become a film star, and second, to write a Yorùbá novel 'like James Hadley Chase'. He did indeed write a novel in Yorùbá, and had the manuscript in his box. Sunday, then, was galvanised by a powerful desire not just for educational qualifications but for a prominent role in a world of literate culture; but this aspiration did not involve a rejection of the Yorùbá language, of indigenous poetic repertoires, or of live performance. Though 'writing' was the idiom in which Sunday spoke of his creative activities, it was a writing that was inseparable from informal learning and from oral improvisation.

Writing, improvisation and the production of a play

The only piece of writing that normally entered into the actual production of a play in the 1980s, when I worked with the Oyin Adéjobí Company, was a synopsis. The idea of the synopsis came from television: the T.V. producers demanded plot outlines, in advance, of every proposed episode of the theatre company's unscripted comedy series such as *Kóòtù Aṣípa* and *Ilé-ìwòsàn*. When they were rehearsing, this synopsis, written by Oyin Adéjobí himself, and typed up by a young girl acting as secretary, seemed to be referred to only once: at the first meeting, when Adéjobí - glancing occasionally at the typed page - explained the story of the play to the assembled company.

What happened after that was the following. The synopsis, which was usually partially but not fully divided into scenes, would be taken over by Alhaji Kàrímù Adépòjù, Adéjọbí's Manager since the 1960s and his right-hand man. Alhaji worked on the story in order to realise it as enactable sequences, marked by exits, entrances, and scene-divisions. He would explain the sequence of events in each scene to the actors. The experienced actors would sometimes make suggestions and additions, but the overall direction of the dialogue was always guided by Alhaji. There were sequences which were carefully orchestrated and rehearsed so that a pattern of statements and counterstatements culminated in an extremely well-controlled, often humorous - indeed hilarious - effect. There were 'landmark' phrases and sentences which endured over the years even when substantial changes in characterisation and plot had occurred. There were 'set pieces' - usually monologues, where one actor took over the microphone and assumed complete control - and also fluid passages between set pieces, where actors navigated their way using the key phrases as landmarks. The actors themselves, especially the more experienced ones, contributed much of the actual dialogue. Each actor tended to excel in certain types of part, and though all insisted that any part could be played by any actor, audience recognition tended to reinforce the association of certain character types with certain actors. The play, they say, becomes 'fuller' in performance. As Alhaji put it:

> Let's say we compose a play now and we give a performance
> one day. Through the audience reaction, or some of them will
> tell us suggestions, or through their reaction, whether the play
> is good or it's not good enough, that will give us - to improve
> the idea or the acting... Immediately I got the idea I will call
> them, 'You did it this way before, we don't want it that way. Do
> it another way'. And I will tell him the way, or tell her the way,
> he will do it. That is how we do our play.

Large scale changes could be made. This could happen gradually, over a long period, as happened with the shedding of the songs in *Kúyẹ̀* - one of the company's oldest plays, which used to be 'all songs, nothing but songs from beginning to end', as Grace Ọ̀wọ́lá, Adéjọbí's senior wife and leading lady, put it. By the 1980s, certain key passages remained in the form of choral song, but most of the dialogue had been converted to naturalistic speech (a change which Grace regretted, but which Adéjọbí regarded as a sign of progress). Big changes could also been installed overnight - as when, in 1983, Adéjọbí and Alhaji became dissatisfied with the ending of their new play *Ọkọ Ìyàwó* and decided to reinforce the moral by adding a whole extra scene in which the anti-heroine, a domineering 'cash madam', is punished by being driven irreversibly mad.

But the plays were also structured to accommodate continuous smaller-scale changes. Many sequences consisted of repeated episodes involving a series of characters. At the beginning of *Àjàgbé Ejò* [Articulated Lorry] the rich landlord summons his tenants to announce the new rules of the house. This speech - a 'set-piece' which the actor (Adéjọbí himself) had completely under his control as long as he was in possession of the microphone - was then responded to by each tenant in turn. More tenants could be added as extra actors became available (I was one such), each making a different set of comic comments on the landlord's equally comic proposals. In *Ìtójúu Kúnlé*, there is a scene in a clinic where the protagonist's wife, presumed drowned, is discovered being given treatment for shock. Her appearance is preceded by a string of other patients, each with a comic or topical complaint. At the beginning of *Fọlájiyọ̀*, a newly-installed and tyrannical oba summons his chiefs one by one to ask them their functions in the town. Each explains his or her particular role, and the oba then abuses, threatens and drives them out on the flimsiest of grounds. In a performance I recorded in 1981, there were five chiefs: Jagun, Ọ̀tún Ìyálóde, Àró Ìlú, Ìyá Awo, and Ìyálóde. In 1988, when I recorded the play again, there were three chiefs: Jagun, Akọgun, and Ìyálóde. Adéjọbí and Alhaji were inventive in creating extra parts on the spur of the moment to accommodate any talent that happened to come their way (the Ọ̀tún Ìyálóde part, for instance, was added for me). When the extra performers were no longer available, it was easy to remove those parts without damaging the overall design of the plot. The structure of the plays facilitated and positively invited additions and alterations in these relatively free-standing repeated dramatic 'slots'.

Within the expansible framework of the plot, each actor gradually consolidated and filled out his or her part. In the earlier version of *Fọlájiyọ̀*, each chief's speech in the opening scene was relatively short and unadorned. By 1988, their speeches were much more elaborate and more differentiated from each other. This is a translation of Chief Jagun's dialogue with the oba in the earlier recording:

Ọba: You who are staring about so foolishly, with eyes like...
      like a bullfrog's, what is your title?
Jagun: Your majesty, may your crown remain long on your
       head, may your shoes remain long on your feet. It
       is I, Jagun, that you see before you.
Ọba: Jagun!
Jagun: I'm the Jagun of this town.
Ọba: What kind of title is Jagun?
Jagun: Ha, if war comes, I am the one who will fight,
       I'm the one who will lead the fighters, if war
       breaks out in this town.
Ọba: You are the one who will fight...?

Jagun: Yes, your majesty. A cutlass is male! If war
        arrives, I'll be ready.

Ọba *(he grabs Jagun and pushes him over):* Look at the Jagun
        of the town, look at the Jagun of my town. This
        is Jagun. This Jagun, I only had to raise my hand
        and he fell down. That's the Jagun of this town.
        Look, from today onwards, if I hear that anyone
        is still calling you Jagun, you'll be in trouble.
        If I hear so much as "Ja - "! If anyone calls you
        Jagun, you will be in debt. And I'm not letting
        you go back to your house. You'll stay at my
        palace, and you'll be one of the people who live
        at the palace and cut grass for my horses. Go on!
        Take him inside! Take him inside!

Seven years later, the Jagun had considerably expanded his part. Rather than
a bare formulaic exchange, there was a more fluid interaction, involving the other
chiefs:

Jagun   *(coughs)*: Hu-hu.
Ọba: May that cough kill you.
Chiefs: Amen, amen.
Ọba: Are you one of the chiefs? What is your title?
Jagun: Your Majesty, it is Jagun.
Ọba: What is your function in the town?
Jagun: It's a hereditary position, is Jagun, because at
        the time of the Kábá war, my forefathers were
        warriors.
Ìyálóde:That's true.
Jagun: At the time of the Àgbádáìgì war, my forefathers
        were war-leaders, in those far-off days. They
        made war, they were victorious. And when my
        father passed away, they said I was to inherit
        his position.
Ìyálóde:Your Majesty, just as your family inherits the
        position of ọba.
Ọba *(sarcastically)*: Thanks for the explanation. And how
        many wars have you yourself fought in?
Jagun: Ha, Your Majesty, ha, in the time since I
        ascended to my father's place, and became chief
        Jagun, there hasn't been any war. But if a war

15

	did break out, Your Majesty, you'll see that a cutlass is male!
Ọba:	Are you saying you wouldn't be able to fight?
Jagun:	Is there anything the matter with me? Ha! What is there to prevent me from fighting? Ha, Your Majesty, is it a fight or a dispute? [i.e. I'm ready for any kind of battle]
Ọba:	Ho! Ho! You are in trouble.
Jagun:	Your Majesty.
Ọba:	You're in trouble. May death strike you down.
Jagun:	Your Majesty.
Ọba:	Well, what's the matter with you? If I hear the name 'Jagun' again, death will strike you down. If I hear 'Jagun', I'll give you cassava-meal mixed with cement to eat. To punish you for the lies you told - *(pushes him over)* look at the Jagun of the town, I just touched him and he fell flat on his face!
Jagun:	I didn't tell any lies.
Ọba:	You're not going back to your house. You'll stay at my palace and cut grass for my horses.
Jagun:	Oh, but I have a wife at home, I have children.
Ọba:	You'll die in the bush.
Jagun:	Oh, I'm in trouble.
Ọba:	Both you, and the wives and children you say you have.
Jagun *(terrified)*:	I didn't say I had any children.
	(He is driven into the Palace chamber)

In this more garrulous rendering, the ọba has become more ferocious, emitting death-dealing curses, and Jagun has become more of a figure of fun. The structure of the episode is the same - it begins with the ọba asking the chief to identify himself, and ends with him threatening the chief and driving him out of the room - and there are enduring key phrases by which the actors keep their bearings: 'A cutlass is male!'; 'If I hear "Jagun" again -'; 'You'll stay at my palace and cut grass for my horses'. In the second version, the ọba brings in a phrase that appears elsewhere in the play in both versions: the threat to give people 'cassava-meal mixed with cement' to eat. This threat was so amusing to the audience that it became a kind of slogan which the actor, John Adéwuni, repeated more and more frequently during the life of the play.

The play, then, was structured to accommodate additions and switches - both improvised and planned - and it gradually became more elaborated, sometimes to the point where it got too long, and entire episodes had to be lopped off to cut it down to size again. This happened through the actors' desire to expand their roles, fuelled by the audience's response, as well as through deliberate thought, planning and experimentation by Adéjọbí and Alhaji, sometimes incorporating the advice of the actors, friends or members of the audience.

The imagined script

When they talked to me about the production process, however, neither Adéjọbí, nor Alhaji, nor the other actors, stressed the oral, improvisatory, collaborative and expansive aspects of their work. Instead, they all insisted on the idea of authorship and writing.[4] The start of the production of a new play, according to Adéjọbí, began with his own solitary reflection upon a story he had heard, read or otherwise acquired. In the case of the Èkùró Ọlọ́jà, he said:

> The story was first told by my late father. I was then still going to school. Because my father used to tell stories - especially when matter happens - that dealt with the necessity for somebody to be loyal, to be sincere, to be truthful. When my father was addressing people generally, or his children, he first told me - told us - told the story, not told me or any other person - he first told the story and I listened well to that story, what he was saying. Then, I never thought I would become somebody who would be writing plays at all. But the story interested me so much, and I was thinking all the time about it. 'So, it is possible for a man to think of something that does not belong to him or her! Á-à-á!' So, but it occurred to me that I should write a play, about twenty years ago [i.e. c. 1968] then I kept off myself from the house, I went somewhere, I sat down, I took my paper and biro, and I first wrote up the story. It was the story I wrote down I started to read over and over and over again. So, after - when I got the play, I assembled my people and told them the story, I told them that I would plan it out. I planned it out, and I presented what I planned out to them.

Adéjọbí's father originally told the story, then, and Adéjọbí's creative process culminated in his re-telling the story to his company: but the emphasis in his

17

account is on the intervening stage, when he closeted himself, alone, with 'paper and biro', and subjected the story to intensive writing, reading over, and ratiocination.

Alhaji said, 'Baba [Adéjọbí] gives me the story, and I turn it into a play'. I asked him how he did this, for I had often been impressed by the way he seemed to have an inner vision of the entire, complex sequence of action and dialogue that made up these three-hour dramas. Alhaji's first response was 'I cannot explain that much because I can say it's God's gift.' However, he went on to talk about the way he saw the process:

> Let's say I have got an idea now, and let's say Baba writes the play, he tells me the story, immediately he's telling me the story I started to read it in my head, and I was seeing it, the way how to direct it.

Alhaji thus combines, with perfect harmony, ideas of telling and ideas of writing. He uses the words synonymously. Baba 'writes the play', which is to say he 'tells me the story'; as he tells him the story, Alhaji starts to 'read it in my head', which enables him to 'see it, the way how to direct it'. He then thinks over what he has been told, working on it in his head:

> This is the way I did it. Let's say I was told the story, and I left that place immediately. On my way to anywhere I'm going, I started to remember, think over, 'How can we do this?' Before I go round and come back I should have collected the way we can do it and how we can do it, that it should be publicly well.

Alhaji thus saw himself as assembling a comprehensive scheme of dramatic dialogue and action on his own, before he began work with the company. When he took the actors through the play in rehearsal, he certainly seemed to be referring to a mental script. With the experienced actors, he would give them key lines and organise the order in which they were to make their points; with the inexperienced ones, he would sometimes teach them what to say line by line. During actual performances, I would sometimes see him walking up and down behind the scenery, correcting actors and giving them cues in a penetrating undertone.

The actors were clearly aware of the enormous importance of their own improvisatory collaboration: they all stressed the value of 'experience', as well as suggesting that only people with certain reservoirs of personality could undertake certain kinds of part: 'You have to be strong to play the Ìyálóde; she's a tough character, not just anyone can do it'. But when they described the production of a play, they overwhelmingly used the vocabulary of instruction and correction. They all took it for granted that there was a blueprint, a right way to do it, and that a good actor is one who can quickly 'catch up', as one actress said, and who does not insist that his/her own way of doing it is better. Abíọ́dún Ọdẹ́jìnmí, a small-part actor on the fringes of the company, explained how actors ought to behave in the following terms:

> [what is good is] if we're told to come, and we all assemble, so, everything they want to say to us about the play we're doing, where each person has to correct his/her mistakes, if they tell the person, and s/he accepts gladly without arguing. Other people will come who, if they make a mistake somewhere in the play, a mistake that they point out to him, when they tell him to correct it he doesn't accept. He'll say the way he does it is better. But the correction they're putting forward is actually better than the way he is doing it. So, what's good is if they tell us something, and we accept it and do it that way. [My translation].

Emily Adéjọbí, one of Adéjọbí's wives and an actress of fourteen years' standing, spoke in terms even more strongly redolent of the schoolroom:

> Before we go to the town where we're going to perform, we'll first assemble on the premises [Adéjọbí's house] in Òṣogbo, the boss will tell us which play we're going to do. The Manager will teach each of us. If he teaches us in the morning, from about nine o'clock to twelve, anybody who still doesn't know his own [part], they'll tell us to meet at five o'clock in he evening. We could still be there till seven or eight, they won't let us go until we know it. [My translation.]

All the participants in the production process, then, talked as if there were a text. It is a text that can be improved and filled out over time, in response to audience reactions. Some people - Adéjọbí and Alhaji - have a more complete grasp of this text than the others, and their role is to 'teach', 'tell' or 'explain' it to the actors until they 'know' it. These improvised plays, then, did seem to be constituted in relation to an imagined script.

Writing and the running of the company

This central but incomplete function of literacy - an absence which oriented all that they did - was played out in the entire operation and organisation of the theatre company. The actual written texts that intervened in the production process - as opposed to the imagined script referred to by Adéjọbí, Alhaji and the company - were apparently peripheral to the drama, but they were given great prominence in the company's own accounts of the process of staging a show. They included the tour itinerary, typed up by the secretary with several carbon copies; the letter of invitation, usually delivered in person by the representative of a social club or other élite group that wished to invite the company to perform; and the posters, which were taken to the towns on the itinerary a few days in advance to advertise the forthcoming show. The letter of invitation was often given prominence in Oyin Adéjọbí's introductory remarks. Introducing the play *Lániyọnu* once, he said:

> Welcome to this evening's entertainment. I don't know what name I ought to give it [i.e. the play], but as far as our theatre company is concerned, 'all snakes are for eating'. I've noticed that three different plays have been publicised [lit.: 'are on paper']. One play is mentioned in the letter of invitation. Another is advertised in the public posters. But the one that they [the Inner Circle Club] told us about, and which we wanted to refuse to do - why? because it's bigger by far than the other two - that one is *Ọlániyonu*. [My translation.]

Note that in the act of foregrounding the letter and the posters - announcements that are 'on paper' and which involve him in a world of literacy - Adéjọbí shows that these written documents commit the company to very little. The suggestion which was actually effectual was the one that they 'bá wa sọ': told us about in speech. The company, however, often talked as if the posters were the most crucial component in the whole business of preparing a new play. I once asked how a new play was coming along. 'When will it be ready?' 'It's almost ready' Emily replied, 'we're just waiting for the posters to come from the printer.' But once, when they could not afford to print a new set of posters, they simply changed the title of their current play so that they could use up an excess stock of old ones. Word of mouth informed the audience what the play would actually be about: and as the company's touring itineraries were very varied, there was little danger that the audience would have seen either of the plays anyway.[5] Similarly, venues and even dates announced on the posters were sometimes changed if bookings fell through or other problems arose, and it was taken for granted that the would-be audience would easily find out the new venue or date by asking around.

Written documents were also given a central position in the company's practices of recruitment, rehearsal and remuneration. An aspiring actor was expected to write a letter of application to the Boss. After the letter of application there was an interview. Yémisí was a Modern School leaver who failed to gain admission to a Training College, decided to try the theatre instead, and later became Adéjọbí's youngest wife. This is how she joined the company:

> I wrote an application. And he asked about my situation. He asked where I come from. I said I came from Òṣogbo. He asked who my parents were, and I explained to him. And then they accepted me. [My translation.]

The application, then, appeared to function primarily as a proof of the applicant's familiarity with formal uses of literacy. The oral interview established the town and family origins of the applicant - criteria which were crucial in identifying people socially. The real audition came only when the applicant actually began to 'practise' and to perform on stage, for it was then that his or her acting ability was assessed for the first time.

The members of the company were paid a monthly salary at a fixed level, which was gradually raised as the actor gained experience and 'long stay'. The payments would be made formally, and the actors would write receipts for the management:

> And we have a way of distributing the money, and we have something that everyone will write, saying that I have received my money this month. We have a 'receipt' thing. If Baba arrives now, everyone will sign in front of him that 'I've received my money, I've received mine.' If they pay the salary today and it happens that there's someone who hasn't time to come until tomorrow, he'll get his money tomorrow and he'll acknowledge then that 'I've received my salary'. [My translation.]

The payment of a monthly salary was an emulation of bureaucratic practice that did not come naturally to all the members of the company. Hamed Akínwálé, a young man employed as a driver by the company who also aspired to be an actor, left the company after a few months because 'at that time, I wasn't used to monthly-paid work, I'd never worked for monthly pay, I was just used to doing a day's work and getting paid that very day. But then I joined another company, and they paid salaries monthly as well, so little by little I got used to it.' However, the formality of the procedures was not matched by the regularity of the company's takings, and there were many months when salaries were late or held over to the following month: a situation that was compensated for by the distribution of bonuses to actors who had done especially well in the good months.

Similarly, the rehearsal schedule imitated the timetable of office work. It was important to the actors to be seen to be working at a regular and respectable profession. They would be required to assemble at the Adéjọbí house every day at 9.00 a.m. even when no rehearsal was planned. As John Adéwuni put it:

> You see, now, when we who aren't natives of this town, who are not natives of Òṣogbo, when we're in the house, those of us who are living together in the house, each one will say s/he is going to his/her place of work, and if you don't say you too are going to your place of work, won't they despise you for that? [laughs] Every day, at nine o'clock, we have to be here. [My translation.]

Non-natives of a town, people who live as tenants, are usually people who have been posted there as teachers or minor civil servants, and who observe formal-sector hours and discipline. As these remarks of John's indicate, there was more at stake than just the usefulness of literacy and bureaucratic regimens in the company's operations. What was at stake was assimilation into a distinctive social sphere, access to which was normally determined by level of education.

Enlightenment, tradition and the public

What, then, does this theatre tell us about the nature and constitution of the 'public' in colonial and post-colonial western Nigeria? It is clear that this is only partly a 'reading public', but more comprehensively a public informed by the idea of reading. We do not know how many primary school leavers, like Sunday Fágbáyìímú, pore over published texts of *ewì*. We do know that the domain of popular entertainment is one that provides oral performative correlates of many written texts. Themes and motifs circulate in and out of print. Some popular plays, for example, are based on stories taken from the famous series of school readers, *Ìwé Kíkà*. One of the Adéjọbí Company's most popular plays is *Kúyẹ̀*, based on a Yorùbá-language novel of the same name by J.F. Ọdúnjọ. Conversely, orally-generated dramas find written representation as photoplay stories in *Atóka*, and sometimes as published plays intended to be read as literature rather than acted. You can read *Kúyẹ̀* as a novel, see it on stage, watch it on television, and read a version extrapolated from the stage play in *Atóka*. You can listen to Dúró Ládiípọ̀'s

Ọba Kò So on LPs, watch it on video or read it in a bilingual edition.[6] You can read his main source (Hethersett's early school reader, *Ìwé Kíkà Ẹ̀kẹrin*), and you can hear variant forms of the *oríkì* (praise poetry) and *ọfọ̀* (incantations) - which constitute much of the text - performed outside the popular theatre domain altogether, in festivals and ceremonies in northern and central Yorùbáland.

Adéjọbí himself placed emphasis on the idea that the theatre offers a powerful and accessible alternative to print media:

> Theatre is so important to the people of our country - specially Yorùbáland - because I regard the practitioners as practical journalists. If you are a journalist you make the report in the paper. Not many people read the paper, and if they read it, they read it for reading's sake. But just imagine putting on the stage the story of an ọba who misused his position - you see - so, there are messages that our people collect from our plays.

A member of the audience I talked to - a young woman - confirmed that 'there are messages' that people 'collect' from the plays. *Èkùrọ́ Ọlọ́jà* is a play about a competition for chiefly title, in which the dishonest candidate almost gets in by cheating, but is exposed at the last minute by his uncompromising former friend, making way for the honest candidate to take the title. She said, 'They did *Èkùrọ́ Ọlọ́jà* on television at the time of Shagari's second government - it was as if they knew what was going to happen'.[7]

The point, then, is not just a historical or genealogical one, about the way the theatre grew out of the church and the schools, with their deep commitment to literacy. It is also a point about how the theatre understood and defined itself. The theatre, in its organisation, its practice, and its individual members' self-conceptions, projected and understood itself as part of a culture of 'enlightenment' defined by literacy, while still accommodating high levels of semi-literacy or illiteracy. 'Not many people read the newspapers', and the strength of the theatre is that it offers an allotrope of written media. It is a genre that aspires to the prestige of the literate world without actually requiring the practitioners and audiences to read, and without sacrificing the flexibility and living immediacy of speech.

Virtual literacy was an excellent platform from which to undertake the selective recuperation, amalgamation and transformation of available ideologies - taken-for-granted ideas which were nonetheless often violently contradictory. In the idiom of a 'writing' which did not permanently fix any text, the intermediate classes could recycle and give a new lease of life to the long-existing narratives, poetic forms and performances now called *àṣà ìbílẹ̀* ('traditional customs'). They could provide a space in which *òrìṣà*, diviners, witches and the ideas and genres associated with them could be given the oxygen of a new publicity. Real drummers would be invited on stage to drum; apprentices who had learnt incantations or *ìjálá* from real oral masters could make their living on the popular stage. 'Writing' these traditions in the medium of the theatre elevated and sanitised them: they were 'our Yorùbá heritage', requiring serious investigation and research before the play could be staged, rather than the 'pagan superstitions' of 'raw illiterates'. In this, of course, the popular theatre producers were following in a long tradition of 'writing culture', which had been pioneered by the Lagosian élite of the late 19th century, and particularly by clergymen such as James Johnson, Samuel Johnson, and E.M. Lijadu. In the act of celebrating local, indigenous traditions the popular theatre people could thus align themselves with a class perceived as superior by virtue of its close links with Western, colonial culture. The idiom of writing simultaneously made room for the continuation of old practices and the claim that here was something new, something modern and progressive - something which transcended and superseded the very traditions they lauded, and which provided a standpoint outside them.

Literacy stands for 'progress' in a double sense. It facilitates an individual's *ìlọsíwájú* - 'moving forward' - in a career, securing better jobs and higher status. But it also represents *òlajú* - 'enlightenment' - in the more general sense of modernity. *Òlajú* is usually used positively to evoke a decent, well-run society, with electricity, hospitals, schools, Christianity, and so on. Literacy or, more generally, schooling, is thus often used as a metonym for an entire cultural and moral order.[8] Claims to superior enlightenment are a powerful weapon in the struggle for social standing. They were particularly useful to the theatre company members who, as they themselves frequently complained, were unfairly regarded by sections of the public as 'vagrants, drunkards, children whose parents have rejected them, smokers of marijuana, people who play while other people are working'. It was partly to counteract this that the theatres laid so much stress on their socially useful role, as 'practical journalists' but even more as 'preachers' teaching moral lessons. They laid claim to a position from which they were responsible for educating their audience. Adédùnmọ́lá, Adéjọbí's eldest daughter, pulled off a neat piece of one-up-womanship in her exposition of the way theatre companies were treated. 'Many people aren't yet enlightened enough to realise that theatre people are respectable people, that they're not people who have been rejected by their parents... They don't realise. It's a form of ignorance.'

The powerful, if unstable accommodation conducted within this framework of *àṣà ìbílẹ̀* and *òlajú* generates cultural effects of remarkable impact. The sphere within which the popular theatre operates is notable for its simultaneous sense of incompletion or lack - a consciousness that there is more schooling, which they do not have, and which opens the way to more influence and more prestige - and its extraordinary, vital self-confidence. After all, out of this sector of the population, marked by its thwarted desire to go to Grammar School and to University, burst a

24

gigantic explosion of creativity - a hundred theatre companies, dozens of 'ewì exponents', a hugely successful outpouring of popular music, hundreds of Yorùbá language novels and volumes of drama and poetry. The theatre reveals its creators' wish to transcend the limitations of the social milieu in which they operate. But aspiration co-exists with confidence in existing cultural practices, and a certain mockery and distrust of the educated élite. The concept of òlajú itself is sometimes used, apparently without irony, to denote the forces that destroyed 'respect for tradition' and 'fear of wrong-doing' (see also Peel, 1978) - an indication that the amalgam of ideas about progress and tradition is always unstable, leaving room for contradiction and internal criticism. No play in the Adéjọbí repertoire actually portrays highly-educated people as objects of unqualified admiration. In Àjàgbé Ejò, the young English-speaking graduate whose aim in life is to do post-graduate studies is treated with derision as well as sympathy. He is an oddity. He has been to England and can criticise Nigerian arrangements (clientilist politics, arranged marriages) from an external perspective; but he is hopelessly incompetent in dealing with the wiles and pressures of the tougher, cleverer, uneducated women around him. In the end he has to be rescued by the common sense of the landlord, a character who - like the majority of actors and theatre-goers - can read a newspaper but is not highly educated. Though Adéjọbí wanted his daughter Adédùnmọlá to go to University and study music or drama there, he was not at all in awe of the university theatre staff. 'Unlike them, we are professionals,' he said, 'we know what our audiences want.'

The representation of literacy and enlightenment was, then, in some ways an ambiguous and contradictory one. But there is no doubt of its powerful pull. The nostalgic affirmation that makes 'orality' the guarantor of 'tradition', 'authenticity' or 'identity' was not shared by the performers or audiences of the Yorùbá popular theatre. They talked about the value of 'our traditions' and even 'our Yorùbá heritage', but never about the value of 'orality'. It was as if the 'Yorùbá heritage' actually appeared to better advantage in the guise of 'writing'. That this orientation is historically and locally specific is demonstrated by strongly contrasting cases in other social and political contexts in colonial Africa: for instance, the long contest for power which took place between 'oral chiefdoms' and 'literate bureaucracies' in the Transvaal, in which, Isabel Hofmeyr tells us, writing was clearly perceived by both sides as an instrument of domination, orality as a form of 'cultural resistance of a community against colonial domination', and their interpenetration the outcome of a political struggle (Hofmeyr 1994). In western Nigeria, on the contrary, the dissolution of boundaries between the 'oral' and the 'written' in popular culture was the outcome of aspiration to a better life. This shows the limitations of the notion of 'hybridity' as an explanatory or even a descriptive category: without a sense of what these fusions and dissolutions mean to the people concerned, and with what intent they were undertaken, the idea of hybridity tells us little.

What needs to be further investigated, however, is the social history of the popular aspiration to 'enlightenment' in western Nigeria; how it has informed everyday experience; and what role it has played in the formation of a public whose consciousness and characteristics can certainly not be predicted from the mere presence of print, the theatre, and the electronic media.

---

1   But see Peel (1968, 1983), Gutkind (1975), Lawuyi (1988), Waterman (1990).

2   In the two cocoa-farm villages studied by Sara Berry (1985), 60% of the grown-up children of the cocoa farmers had moved into the tertiary sector, the majority of them into trading, artisanal jobs or transportation.

3   *S'àgbà di wèrè*, by Ọlánrewájú Adépọjù, Oníbọnòjé Press, Ìbàdàn, 1972.

4   Just as those who were fluent in English preferred to use English in interviews I recorded with them (though we spoke Yorùbá to each other all the time otherwise), so it is quite possible that they stressed the importance of writing more in these interviews than they would have done in other contexts. I was from the University of Ifẹ̀, and was writing a book about the theatre company, which may have made people feel they should present their work in as 'progressive', 'educated' a light as possible. However, the very fact that I, an academic, was eagerly incorporated into the company, and my participation announced and advertised at every opportunity, was indicative of a positive orientation towards the sphere of education. Mr Adéjọbí was enthusiastic about the idea of having a book written about him and his company, and also wanted the texts of his plays to be published. It is also important to note that the foregrounding of the idea of written texts did not occur only in interviews with me: it went on in many dimensions of their actual theatrical practice, as will be seen below.

5   This was only possible with new and relatively unknown plays, however. Some of their older plays - especially those which had been shown on television - were so famous and so beloved by audiences that they could not possibly have used their titles for other plays without causing disappointment and outrage among their fans.

6   Ládiípọ̀ was exceptional in being supported and sponsored by Ulli Beier and then by the Institute of African Studies at Ìbàdàn University. The publication of *Ọba Kò So*, *Ọbá Wàjà* and *Ọbá Mọ́rọ̀* was undertaken by the Institute and the transcriptions and translations of the texts were prepared by Institute staff. However, this exercise in publication was in no way an alien 'scriptocentric'

intrusion. Many theatre companies aspired to publish versions of their plays; Adéjọbí himself said he had two ambitions: to make a film, and to publish some of his favourite plays.

7   Shagari's party, the NPN, was widely regarded in western Nigeria as having massively rigged the 1983 elections which gained it a second term of office. Disgust and anger were widespread until January 1, 1984, when Shagari's government was overthrown by a military coup led by Buhari.

8   In J.F. Ọdúnjo's *Ọmọ Òkú Ọrun* (1964), for example - a novel whose plot the Adéjobí Theatre borrowed for their play *Ìtọ́júu Kúnlé* - there is a greedy, unscrupulous and cruel step-mother character who worms her way into the household of a widower who moves in more educated circles than she does. The novel suggests that her lack of education makes her not only lazy, vulgar and unkind, but also incompetent at housekeeping! Cleanliness, Godliness and common kindness are here conflated under the sign of education.

Myth, Ritual and Song as 'Counter Texts' in three plays of Derek Walcott

Nana Wilson-Tagoe

Each time we try to express ourselves
We have to break with ourselves
                              Octavio Paz

Paz's statement enacts a linguistic and dialectical dilemma in all post-colonial writing. The agonising conflicts that arise within discourses of self-definition expressed in the given languages of colonial cultures are evident in the often tortuous relationships between thought and language in the literature of ex-colonial societies. European languages are steeped in European thought, and European thought through centuries of colonisation rationalised an ideology of dominance which not only defined 'the other' in a hierarchically organised relationship but also controlled and manipulated the naming of things and systems of knowledge. For ex-colonial writers the processes of re-definition and the creation of a new consciousness and authority necessitate an imaginative re-positioning and interrogation of European knowledge and systems as well as a continual subjectification and self-formation.

For the Caribbean writer this imaginative activity is made more complex by the very nature of colonial reality in the Caribbean and by the fact that as colonials' both master and slave were engaged in a reciprocal relationship that shaped their lives[1]. Within this context the Caribbean writer's re-definition often moves beyond manichean oppositions to grapple with all aspects of this reality, descending, in Wilson Harris's words;

> beneath the surface mind of a culture into other structures that
> after emphases upon vague and elusive formations suppressed
> by static gestalt institutions.[1]

Such descents and explorations have enabled writers to respond in subtle ways to inarticulate layers of Caribbean space and to variables of myth and legend generated by displaced people in the region. The efforts of perception and the imaginative correlations involved in these confrontations has generated a new radical art whose energies not only interrogate and destabilise European conceptualisations about the region but also deflate the tyrannical hold of the written word, creating new ways of seeing, new myths and a whole new corpus of sensibility.

The orientation has grown out of a gradual deconstruction of the notion of individual agency in the region and from an appreciation of an oral world of tradition and expression capable of mediating between text and speech and between the writer and his/her community. It shows itself as a movement from a focus on text to a focus on communication and has been more radical in drama than in poetry and fiction.

The tensions between a poet's constructed text and his wish to be truthful to the inner life of his community are for instance, constantly enacted in Walcott's poetry and may explain the marked difference between his relation to language in poetry and drama. In his early poetry Walcott had been inclined towards metaphor and paradox as a source of meaning and had constantly sought:

> the paradoxical flash of an instant in which every facet
> was caught in a crystal of ambiguities.[2]

Throughout his poetry this imaginative urge to heighten, recreate and extend life through metaphor and paradox had clashed with a personal need to be true to his landscape and people, and although Walcott appears to accept this tension as an energising force in his poetry[3] his relation to myth, ritual and song in the dramatic mode reveals the extent to which it had pushed him towards drama and theatre. It seems to me that an examination of the changed relationship between Walcott and his text in drama should reveal the various creative ways in which an oral tradition may energise the imagination and deflate the power of the written word as a single totalising mode of perception and signification.

Walcott's own articulation of the distancing between language and life in his poetry should present a revealing starting point:

> Years ago, watching them, and suffering as you watched, you
> proffered silently the charity of a language which they could
> not speak, until your suffering, like your language, felt
> superior, estranged. The dusk was a raucous chaos of curses
> gossip and laughter, everything performed in public, but the
> voice of the inner language was reflective and mannered as
> far above its subjects as that sun which would never set until
> its twilight became a metaphor for the withdrawal of Empire
> and the beginning of our doubt.[4]

It was obviously his awareness of this distance and his personal and artistic need to bridge its gap that influenced Walcott's desire to create 'not merely a play but a theatre, not merely a theatre but its environment'.[5] For in relation to the connotations of 'play', 'theatre' and 'theatrical environment' text as we understand it changes in various ways. In drama and theatre the poet-dramatist moves from a hermetic world of allusive representation and flashes of ambiguity into a wider dramatisation of human action and its reverberations in human society; and within this public medium metaphor becomes not merely an image of the poet's subjective imagination but also conversation (as it is and has always been for the ordinary people): the tones and inflexions of speech, the implications and associations of symbols and myths. At the same time the dramatist's attempts to create theatre, his enactment of aspects of life, his merging of landscape, people and consciousness in celebration or purgation moves drama into areas where a play becomes a performance, even a ritual, and text is subsumed into the communicative event, deconstructed and made part of other modes of perception and signification.

Myth, ritual and song in Walcott's plays seem to me to enact such a relationship between text and performance though commentators on the plays have not always made much of this. A play like *Ti Jean And His Brothers* which everybody knows is based on a St Lucian folktale and has general mythic extensions, is actually a performance, an enactment of myth that integrates the old myth into consciousness and at the same time extends it to make new ones. Indeed the play recalls Walcott's earlier fascination with the grounded source and mythic possibilities of the St Lucian folktale in a way that gives us several clues about how to approach it.

> A tale that had sprung from the hearthside or lamplit hut-door
> in an age when the night outside was a force, inimical,
> infested with devils, wood-demons, a country for the journey of
> the soul.[6]

Walcott's appropriation of the myth is not just an appropriation of its story, structure and symbol; it is an appropriation of its incantative force as an enactment and purgation of a community's fears and anxieties. His play links itself to the immaterial time of the myth, situates itself within its space and takes on its characters and rituals. Thus aside from the stylised but lyrical language (which Walcott achieved by breaking the iambic line into half to accommodate the lilt of dialect speech), aside from the inner structure and the three moral revelations, there is also the 'counter-text', subsumed in the performance aspect of the play. Here the mythic space becomes a character in the drama, embodying an arena of the unspeaking which characters and audience are continually invited to relate to. It is an enclosed world of forests, animals, men and the elements, an area of wet melancholy mountains, of rain falling hard on leaves or caught in dripping branches; a primordial world in continual metamorphosis where animals eat animals as nature's law demands and where the earth becomes a womb that swallows man. As a source of myth this arena is the site of a metaphysical and political contest (All the brothers have to pass through the bamboo forest, over the black rocks out of the enclosed forest and into the open valley to meet the devil/planter), and throughout the performance the actors within the play, the audience within the play and the play's own audience are continually invited to integrate this space into consciousness as a link with the past and as a source of other myths.

In addition and in keeping with the mobilisation of emotions and energies involved in performance, the play makes direct links at various points, with actors, players and audience, inviting them to participate in the struggle over inimical forces and contradictions as well as the final resolution of Ti Jean's context. In ordinary drama elements of conflict criss-cross and move relentlessly towards a dramatic concentration and a resolution which are presented as a spectacle for the aesthetic enjoyment of an audience. In *Ti Jean* the rituals of myth are part of the inner structure of the play as well as its performance. The frog tells the story as an incantation to persuade the moon to light the evil dark and take away the rain but the animals who are his listeners and audience are continually involved in the dangers, threats and fears experienced by the actors in the story. The old man is at once within and outside the enactment, projected as part of the unheard and unspoken life of the community with a stake in the resolutions of the contest. Thus his song of disappointment at Gro Jean's certain defeat is also a song in anticipation of the mythic hero who can defeat the forces of evil.[7] On those occasions when he becomes part of the enactment he seems to me to function as part of an inbuilt control that enacts the many-faceted nature of evil. His many disguises appear then as mechanisms through which the community initiates the mythical hero into the enigmatic nature of evil whether it resides in the forest or is embodied in the planter. Indeed there are elements of play, suggestion and gentle persuasion in the old man's various disguises (old man of the forest, planter, devil, God) to indicate a paradoxical function and suggest he has as much stake in Ti Jean's victory as the animals.

Laurence Breiner has suggested that *Ti Jean* is a play that selects its own hero, and it seems to me this is a suggestion about the various emotional involvements enacted as part of Ti Jean's contest with evil. For the final contest between Ti Jean and the devil is indeed an elaborate performance in which all the players are implicated. First the drama and the 'Bolom's' song and dance announce the urgency of the journey and what is at stake for the possibility that is unborn; then the metaphysical and political arena are focused upon: the evil dark of the forest where sun and rain contend for mastery, simulating Ti Jean's own contest and leaving the question in balance as to whether he will win with the sun or perish with the rain; and later the political battleground of the sugar estates, the arena of new myths central to the modern audience. Every stage in the performance then becomes a celebration in which emotions are stored by actors

31

and audience. The challenge that Ti Jean poses, his refusal to accept old categories and definitions, the disturbance he causes in the devil/planter and the revolutionary burning of the estates all release energies which reverberate among the actors, animals and audience and which the narrator of the myth extols by deliberately returning into the story to recount the event in epic-like tones (And all night the night burned/Turning on the spit/Until in the valley, the grid/Of the carefield glowed like walls/). On the other hand the final confrontation where it is uncertain whether Ti Jean will succeed becomes another performance in which all characters with stakes in the victory are part of the anxiety and suspense; the Bolom casting himself between Ti Jean and the devil to outline the contest and stake a claim to life; the mother's song and prayer suggesting victory by hinting at Ti Jean's Christ-like and redemptive destiny and the animals entering the contest as a chorus that with Ti Jean and the natural world around, affirms renewal and continuity in the face of evil.

The performance achieves a collective purgation on two fronts. The incantation works; the rain stops; the sun appears and some re-unification is restored, suggesting that renewal is possible. In the modern myth a certain paralysing fear of the planter has been exorcised.

Perhaps it is only in drama and theatre that such descents as Harris talks of may recover visions that may be extended in shared celebration and purgation. The Caribbean writer and critic, Edouard Glissant has noted that as in the unfolding of myth, what theatre expresses in its early stages is not the psychology of a people but its shared destiny through the investigations of why it acts and how its forward movement unfolds. In this unfolding it is the dispersal and linking of emotions achieved through performance rather than the nuances and ambiguities of the constructed text that afford a suitable medium. Glissant's statement may apply in slightly different ways to Walcott's continued myth-making in the plays after *Ti Jeans* even though the forest and its space are still the source of myth. The folkloric material of *Ti Jean* dramatised a different spiritual journey inspired by different threats and fears. Walcott's modern myths are prompted by other anxieties, where in *Ti Jean* actors, players and audience are continually invited to share in the trials, suspense and catharsis of the journey, we have in *Dream on Monkey* mountains individual manifestations of the journey inspired by the same disturbance but internalised and resolved in separate ways, and it is as if in the modern myth Walcott suggests purgation is an individual matter. The epilogue of *Dream* hints at Makak's Messianic and mythic function, a role he acquires because he contends with and exorcises the demons of his disturbance. Yet such a liberation is achieved entirely by Makak alone. His execution of the apparition is his way of coming to terms not only with the failure of his dream but also with the psychic confusion and personal crisis that had inspired his assumed African and European identities. Lestrade never achieves this catharsis though he and others are part of the rituals of the spiritual journey performed. Because purgation is private myth functions as counter text in other ways. The dream itself becomes a large metaphor of disturbance with its source in the psychic that brings on Makak's hallucination. But it is played out in different ways so that it is really only as partakers in the same disturbance that the actors in *Dream* may be in fellowship. Indeed it is possible to see performance here as a big 'mass' in which players act out different roles and rituals from which there may be no liberation.

The carnival songs and dances, the masks and symbols combine to present an atmosphere of spectacle within which the role plays are enacted, and it is from the similar and contrasting performances that the play's statements and epiphanies arise. Makak's rage of the lion is no less a mask than Lestrade's Eurocentricism. Yet within this general mimicry the empowering and healing aspects of the dream remain a referent against which may be measured the perverted parodies of other characters. Thus Makak's genuine ritual of healing is savagely parodied in Moustique's and Tigre's selfish impersonations, just as Lestrade's conversation from 'white' to black become a foil to Makak's true liberation. We have moved away, it seems, from the communal catharsis of the old myth, and Walcott's modern myth is a myth of the lone mythical visionary.

It appears clear now that in Walcott's plays text takes on several aspects as a communicative event rather than a self-contained signifying system. In *Ti Jean* it is subsumed in the performance of myth, In *Dream* it is part of the rituals of role-playing, in *Pantomime* a much later play, it is in fact the performance itself, providing a vehicle for language as song and performance. In all three instances language seems to me to function as a counter-text, providing a vehicle for the expression of a Caribbean mythology or linguistic mode. Yet ironically *Pantomime* is the artists' performance alone (possibly on behalf of his community). Only two characters act out the pantomime of the Crusoe myth, taking on different roles, cutting out, revising and improvising in response to twists in arguments and emotional response, so that playwright, actors and audience are involved in the torture of articulation and in the responsibility of deconstructing the Classic European myth of Crusoe. Because Robinson Crusoe is an archetypal story of imperialism, an engagement with it is an engagement with history, and Walcott's drama examines, discards and adopts various relations to the 'Crusoe' story in search for a creative relation to history in the contemporary situation. The Pantomime turns out not to be a light entertainment but a progressive enactment of the squalidness and violence of colonial relations, giving rise only to feelings of revenge and remorse and demonstrating history as a subjective narrative full of personal crises. In the performance it is only when the actors relate to each other as humans that they achieve an understanding beyond the defined roles of master and servant, and in the process Walcott's performer creates a medium of perceiving and communicating that is native to the Caribbean.

The differentiation made between classical and creole acting creates an idiomatic distinctiveness for Creole as it pits itself against Harry's classical language and classical interpretation of the "Crusoe" text. In using creole as a medium for revision the Walcott's Jackson makes that text native to the Caribbean. Crusoe's creole idiom is for instance, convincingly intertwined with the New World environment and New World consciousness of Jackson in such a way that it sounds so sharply different from the idiom of the classical Crusoe. Walcott it seems to me, suggests that this kind of appropriation involves a great deal of creative perception and interpretation and is not necessarily a form of mimicry, so that in the end, it is possible to 'creolise' the classical "Crusoe" text and by extension, the very history ingrained in it.

In addition to the creole language, the calypso form, with its impromptu elements, improvisation and invention, presents another medium of perception and communication which revises and finally creolises the classical text, giving both actors and audience a personal, distinctive and finally, creative relation to history.

> ... in the Caribbean, we do not pretend to exercise power
> in the historical sense. I think that what our politicians
> define as power, the need for it, should have another
> name: that, like America, what energises our society is
> the spiritual force of a culture shaping itself...[8]

Such a creative process is what is finally, literally enacted at the end of *Pantomime* when as it appears, the two actors, spiritually/emotionally attuned and co-ordinating now, create, impromptu, their panto/caiso:

Jackson:
>   (Through laughter)
>   So... so... next Friday... when the tourists come...
>   Crusoe...
>   Crusoe go be ready for them... Goat race...

Harry: (Laughing)
>   Goat - roti!

Jackson: (Laughing)
>   Grambling.

Harry: (Baffled)
>   Grambling?

Jackson: Goat - to - pack, Every night...

Harry: (Laughing)
Before they goat - to - bed!

Jackson: (Laughing)
So he striding up the beach with is little goatee.

Harry: (Laughing)
E - goat - istical. again.
(pause)

Jackson: You get the idea. So, you okay, Mr Trewe?

Harry: I'm fine, Mr Phillip, You know... (He wipes his eyes).
An angel passes through a house and leaves no imprint of
his shadow on its wall. A man's life slowly changes and he
does not understand the change. Things like this have
happened before, and they can happen again. You
understand, Jackson? You see what it is I'm saying?[9]

Only in drama perhaps, can such an enactment be possible and convincing. It is in the medium of drama more than in poetry that a writer can share in the articulation and purification of the people's speech. Thus whereas in poetry language encapsulates the poet's individual thoughts and his linguistic manipulation of these, in drama the very immediacy of communication demands a different relation to language. There is a great deal of difference for instance, in the conception of metaphor as we experience it in Walcott's poetry and as we experience it in his plays. In the plays metaphor in the context of ordinary speech is conversation not the elaboration of image, and in all his drama Walcott strives to create the precise inflexions of the people's inner language, keeping as close to its tone and strengths as possible and in the process making the language and the oral traditions visible and creative. Thus if in Walcott's poetry we respond to the words and thought processes of the introspective poet, in his drama we are forced to listen to the familiar speech of the people as well as witness the enactment of life through the oral structures and forms that the people have created. In the final analysis it is the separate demands of poetry and drama that creates the differences in thrust and achievement between Walcott's poetry and his drama. His poetry manifests the private introspective imagination of the poet while his drama communicates a sense and feel of tradition and community.

1   Naipaul defines this reciprocal culture as the simplicities of race and money; Lamming sees the 'possibility' beyond these, and Brathwaite adds on another definition: a human and social 'culture' of creolisation.

2   Harris 1981: 131.

3   Walcott 1973: 58.

4   For an explicit statement on this see Walcott 'meanings', *Savacou*, No 2, 1970; and for an interrogation of Walcott's position see Fred D'Aguiar's article: "Ambiguity without a Crisis?" in Stewart Brown (ed.) *The Art of Derek Walcott*.

5   Walcott 1970: 6.

6   Walcott 1970: 24.

7   The Old Man's Song is a lament that stands out against Gros Jean's confident strides and links with the immemorial anxieties and quests to which the myth is linked.

8   Walcott 1974: 3-13.

9   Walcott 1980: 169.

The Satanic Rehearsals:
Devils, Sex and Deviance in Guyanese and Caribbean Popular Theatre

Al Creighton

The main activity in contemporary Guyanese theatre today has very little to do with the major dramatists. Most of the country's best known directors and actors have migrated and the works of the foremost playwrights are only occasionally seen in performance, if at all. Those who have produced the most important plays in terms of publication, performance history, literary and critical acclaim include Michael Gilkes, best known for *Couvade*[1], Michael Abbensettes[2], Frank Pilgrim, best known for *Miriamy*[3], Slade Hopkinson[4], N.E. Cameron[5] and most recently, Harold Bascom who is also a novelist.[6] Gilkes, winner of the Guyana Prize for Drama in 1992[7], returned home that same year after having lived in Barbados since 1974. Abbensettes went to Britain much earlier and now lives in London while Hopkinson has lived in Barbados, Trinidad, Jamaica and Canada.

But with the exception of Bascom, it is not their drama that dominates the Guyanese stage, although Gilkes's revisit of *Couvade* in Georgetown in 1993 received very high acclaim. Several other well known Guyanese plays, including some good work, have been produced by two generations of dramatists whose names are significant; among these are Sheik Sadeek, Bertram Charles and Francis Quamina Farrier, one of the more active playwrights in the 1960's - 70's; and a newer group including Harry Naraine, Hector Jay Bunyan, Ian Valz and Paloma Mohamed who have all had plays on Guyana Prize shortlists. Farrier, whose work includes the patriotic and the historical, and Sadeek have worked in earlier popular vogues while Charles has attempted fairly ambitious investigations into the inherent evil in the mind of man. There is great merit in Bunyan's latest play and in Naraine's which are yet to be staged, but Valz and Mohamed who are part of the prevailing popular movement, are frequently performed.

It took a decade for Guyana to experience the wide ranging popularization of dramatic theatre with the growing emphasis on realism that was taking place elsewhere as Caribbean playwrights intensified their awareness of local audiences and sensibilities. Long after a similar explosion in Jamaica, a fairly new corpus of mainly popular plays of topical and gender issues, domestic intrigue and local street life developed in Guyana in the late 1980's. This theatre is characterized by sexual intrigue, a racy bluntness, colourful language, invocation of evil spirits - mainly obeah - done in theatrical types that emphasize the popular thriller, topical issue, domestic soap opera, melodrama, farce, slapstick and comedy. They are highly commercial plays which communicate mainly by direct appeal to the box office, responding to a popular taste and demand for entertainment of the type usually received from the cinema. The plays represent a new experience for the Guyanese audience; that of seeing real local life and issues presented as the source of those thrills of sensationalism, sex and humour that they associate with imported films, but rendered more hilarious because of the element of familiarity.

The rise of this popularization came relatively late to Guyana just as other advances in modern and post-modernist theatre have done after they developed elsewhere in the Caribbean. In 1981 the newly formed Theatre Company, the first professional company to establish itself in Guyana, launched its activities with a local satirical review titled *The Link Show*. This was a derivative of the *Brink* series co-authored by Frank Pilgrim and produced by the Theatre Guild, the country's leading amateur establishment of which the new company's director Ron Robinson was an executive member. *The Brink* revues, last seen in 1980, reflected the older middle class sophistication of the earlier colonial theatre out of which the Theatre Guild grew and Robinson injected into it jokes, rumours, some sexuality including racy anecdotes from Guyanese street culture to make it the most popular theatrical event in the country with unprecedented box office records. But real satire was sacrificed to a degree and *The Link*'s offerings included ridicule rather than satirical treatment of situations sensationally rendered but really not laughable. The Company, as well as other former members of The Guild, saw to the rise of a commercial theatre with production of new plays mainly by Valz and Leon Saul, which were thrillers with local themes and situations. These were interspersed with imported murder mysteries (including plays by Agatha Christie and Frederick Knott), comedies and farces. As the years progressed, there was a gradual swing towards localization, original local plays and a movement away from the foreign dramas.

The Theatre Guild, which for much of this period still commanded the best talent in the country, insisted through its leaders (foremost director John Rollins, Lennox Foster, Eze Luke and Ulita Anthony) on amateur status, seeking to select scripts for artistic merit rather than box office appeal. The new producers therefore moved to the National Cultural Centre, a larger, more commercial venue with a new emphasis on the popular audience. It was the beginning of an era in which dramatists, actors and producers were able to earn money from their work although much of it is commercial rather than professional. The best new playwrights to emerge at that time were Grace Chapman, Valz and Bascom who pioneered this particular development of Guyanese drama in the decade of the eighties with emphases different from those of their predecessors. Chapman's *The Green Bottle* (1981;revised 1983) started a trend of Guyanese horror thrillers based on obeah and spirit possession which had a number of followers including Valz's *Room to Let* (1983), Michael Duff's *Kathy Ann's Possessed* (1991) and Churaumani

Bissundyal's not so successful *The Migrant Error* (1990), while Bascom's *The Barrel* (1981; revised 1992) opened the way for 'mirror' plays, Guyanese domestic dramas which pointedly present issues and life patterns as they exist at Georgetown 'street' and 'grassroot' level. Although his plays are not comedies - his characters learn bitter lessons in tragic twists at the end - Bascom's earlier dialogues are often weakened by comic lines for popular consumption. But a combination of sensationalism, laughter, melodrama, crowd-pleasing gimmicks and genuine talent helped to make him not only the most popular but the most influential local playwright working in Guyana.

Despite his reputation as a popular dramatist, Bascom can hold a place among the country's better playwrights, having developed away from the temptation of gimmickry into creditable formal development of his morally instructive tragic vision. His best plays, improved by revisions, are important to Guyanese social realism, but the greater impact on Guyanese theatre remains in his influence of and by popular entertainment.

The mass media of cinema and television first provided inspiration for Grace Chapman's drama of demonic possession inflicted on a victim of envy, later taken up by Bascom, Valz, Duff and many lesser talents. The very popular horror films such as *The Exorcist* with their sequels, provided initial stimuli for these plays not only in subject but in style, since several attempts have been made to effect cinematographic techniques on the contemporary Guyanese stage with fluctuating levels of success. In addition to flirtations with stage gimmickry and the limited lighting effects available to assimilate the spectacle of levitation and other phenomena, the popular dramatists inevitably returned to obeah and myal, on-going favourites in Caribbean theatre. They also drew on the mystique surrounding one of the legacies of Dutch colonization: the many legends of demonic spirit possession and the still dreaded reputation of the awesome power of the brand of obeah and necromancy practiced in the times of the Dutch. Some of this has been fictionalized in Mittelholzer's compelling ghost story, *My Bones and My Flute*. Bascom exploited these as much as the others, while setting trends borrowed from the cinema. The local domestic 'soap opera' exhibited likely resonances of the prevailing television serials as he introduced sequels to some of his popular plays. Even his best work, *Philbert and Lorraine* (1992) which examines difficulties surrounding Caribbean migration to the USA often involving 'visa weddings'[8], is sub-titled *Visa Wedding II* after his popular *Visa Wedding* (1989) although the 1992 play is a formidable and successful work in its own right which exists independently of its precursor. Another of his better dramas with a title aimed at the thrill-seeking audience, *Tessa Real Girl and the Old Fool*, (1990; revised 1992) about a street-wise Georgetown 'real girl'[9] who leads men on to exploit them, reflects the possible influence of the Hollywood film *Pretty Woman*. A number of his works, including this one, are worth much more than the crowd-catching titles he gives them.

The use of sequels is taken up by Ronald Hollingsworth as well as by Paloma Mohamed who also exploits the popular while pursuing other interests in her better plays about the destruction of family life by migration (*Mammy*, 1991) and an experiment on the life of Bob Marley (*Reggae Marley*, 1989). Mohamed strongly defends the commercial motivation as necessary activity for dramatists to earn money or to break even. Sure enough, she treats her commercial plays as pot boilers to fund what she considers to be her more serious work. But worthwhile examination of an issue is achieved in only one of Hollingsworth's popular thrillers, *Diplomatic Blow* (1992) designed to seduce the crowds with an offer of the voyeuristic delights of sexual infidelity. Its point of interest where social realism is concerned, is an interesting reversal in the gender-related theme of sexual exploitation in which the predatory male is deluded by what he thinks is a prized conquest but ends up destroyed, ruthlessly exploited by the woman he thought he had conquered. Sexual intrigue, also employed by Mohamed, is however, the primary concern as it is for a number of others such as Vivian Williams, Ken Danns and Ras Michael. The fashionable sexuality comes as much from popular culture as it does from the imported film media, but it lured Ras Michael away from his interesting expositions of ghetto life into two less successful plays and induced a new writer, Lloyd Grannum, into an unsuccessful beginning before he moved into over-telegraphed moralistic dramas.

The Guyanese development followed trends already established in the wider Caribbean, particularly Jamaica where social realism in the theatre had been intensifying since 1970. Around that time there were major breakthroughs for the growing professional industry after the opening of The Barn Theatre by Yvonne Jones Brewster and Trevor Rhone. Rhone's hit *Smile Orange* (1970) and his lesser work *Comic Strip* (1969) helped to lay a strong foundation for theatre which tuned in to the popular audience with plays which succeed in social commentary through popular genres. This helped to make it possible for a commercially viable theatre to develop. The topical issue drama and the domestic realist plays may be exemplified by other Rhone works such as *Sleeper* (domestic), *School's Out* (topical satire) and *Two Can Play* (topical, domestic) as well as by the work of other leading dramatists, Carmen Tipling's *Straight Man* (topical) and *The Skeleton Inside* (topical, domestic), Ginger Knight's *Whiplash* (topical, domestic tragedy) and Basil Dawkin's *Champaigne and Sky Juice* (topical, domestic comedy).

There were a number of worthy counterparts in Trinidad such as *One of Our Sons is Missing* (1991; topical, about AIDS), Raoul Pantin's *Radio Republic 555* (1985) and Mustapha Matura's *The Coup* (1991) both topical satires about corruption and coup d'états. The foregoing, however, are samples from the best products of social realism and the plays that featured in the popularization of the theatre in the Caribbean. Progressively, the region's theatre had grown outside of small colonial middle class dramatic circles to embrace an increasing popular audience. But there were also easier routes for communication with that audience. These were pursued on a large scale after Ed Wallace, a radio morning show host, started a theatre in Kingston which specialized in light comic fare both foreign and local with a primary interest in the box office. Gloudon (1982: 67) complains about

> the advent of a new kind of *quick-stick* commercialism [w]hen Wallace . . . in 1976 . . . proceeded to bring to the public a spate of productions written by new Jamaican playwrights, many working to a formula of *play it for laughs and don't spare the sex*. This formula found great favour with a new audience who flocked to these productions, laughing all the way.[10]

However, the Wallace factor was only the extension of a larger movement of popularization which cannot be all negative despite criticisms of the lack of artistic merit in the 'new' plays. It arose from the continuing demand for a theatre in close touch with its audience, a demand which also produced excellent plays. It is part of a long history of grassroots theatre formerly performed in cinema houses in vaudeville and 'Christmas Morning Concerts' which included comedy teams, humorous skits and improvizations. Out of this came Ed 'Bim' Lewis, formerly a member of the Bim and Bam comedy team, who continued cinema-house performances after the retirement of his partner, creating plays in the manner of the Nigerian Ogunde Theatre. In the beginning plots were sketched out and dialogue improvized by the actors before full scale plays were produced and taken on tours around Jamaica much as the Ogunde did in Nigeria.

Lewis presented a blend of earthy humour and topical issues in his courtroom dramas whose phallic symbolism is reflected in titles such as *The Case of the Bald Head Rooster* and *The Case of the Big Head Walking Stick*. But he graduated to more telling mirrors as in *John Ras I*, exploiting humour from the controversies arising out of the Rastafari in Jamaican society. The pinnacle of his success was reached with *A Gun Court Affair* (1974), a comic musical which cashed in on the very topical and controversial emergency Gun Court set up by the Manley Government to deal with rampant gun crimes. Lewis died at his zenith after seeing *A Gun Court Affair* break box office records as the longest running play in Kingston in the mid seventies. He collapsed backstage during a performance of his most worthwhile play.

The legacy he left includes the roots or dance hall play, sometimes referred to as 'crotch theatre' because of its focus, which developed rapidly in the 1980's. It is reminiscent of the creative deviance earlier evident in the jamette carnival of nineteenth century Trinidad with its defiant sexuality, continuing in some aspects of the calypso culture and in the dance hall 'slackness' of explicit DJ lyrics and sexually charged choreography. Voyeuristic sexual exploits reinforced by slapstick are in the main ingredients in roots in which plot and theme exist just sufficiently to hold sequences of farce together. Activities in the genre have included the conversion of the Regal Cinema by playwright Ralph Holness and the Green Gables from which Balfour Anderson operates into theatres for these plays which are also taken on tour to various locations in Jamaica, while similar plays by counterparts in Britain are performed at small theatres there. Holness, in addition, has now begun filming his plays for video. Other popular theatres such as the Barbadian stand pipe which inspired the 'Talk Tent', Thom Cross's *Laugh it Off* and to a lesser extent, *Bimshire*, are worth mentioning as being obliquely related. But, like the popular domestic melodramas of Antiguan Nambalala, none of these venture into sexuality as directly as the dance hall or as Trinidadian Freddy Kissoon's *Doctor Beulah* plays or his *Calabash Alley*[11] which are closer equivalents of the roots.

A proper analysis of the genesis and place of this theatre for which Cooper[12] is extremely helpful, is beyond the scope of this paper. 'Renegade' theatre such as this and the dance hall creative expression satisfies a demand in the popular arena which reflects significant dimensions of a culture descended from social structures under slavery, in the post-emancipation and colonial periods which consistently worked to condemn and control African masque, music, song and dance. The sexuality as manifested in these, which were vestiges of older traditions of cathartic ritual, were vigorously attacked as vulgar and devilish.

The devil entered the arena from among the earliest comments written by Europeans about the masquerade or jonkunnu in the eighteenth century.

> During Christmas holidays, they have several tall, robust
> fellows dressed up in grotesque habits, and a pair of ox-horns
> on their heads, sprouting from the top of a horrid sort of vizor,
> or mask which about the mouth is rendered very terrific with
> large boar husks. The masquerador, carrying a wooden sword
> in his hand, is followed with a numerous crowd of drunken
> and disreputable women of the town who refresh him
> frequently . . . whilst he dances at every door, bellowing out
> "John Connu !" with great vehemence.

The description is Satanic. It could serve as a portrait of Lucifer himself; but that is how the Europeans saw the masques: as devilish and the 'crowd of disreputable women' is an image that lasted through the times of jamette carnival to the contemporary dance halls. The literature is replete with remarks about the demonic nature of slave, ex-slave and working class performances to the point where sexuality became synonymous with devilry. This equation remains even in contemporary consciousness. The notion is reflected in the image of E.E. Cummings's 'goat-footed balloonman'[13] borrowed from the archetype of the lecherous greek satyrs to symbolize the children's growing into knowledge of the world, sex and age. Set in the 'mud-/luscious' spring season of fertility, this beckoning sexuality which is also the coming of death, (cf. Paradise Lost and Elizabethan/Donnean eroticism) lurks on the edges of the poem in the devilish form of a 'balloonman'. But indeed, devils and demonic masks have been very prevalent throughout the Trinidad carnival as well as in traditional enactments and mummeries across the Caribbean even to the point where devils and outrageous suggestiveness become symbols or trade-marks of defiance used by proletarian masquers against the ruling class or even in battles against each other[14].

Sexual potency, insurrection and rivalry which come together in the kalinda have therefore come to be associated with resistance as well as creative energy (Warner-Lewis, 1991) among the working class who frequent the dance hall and make up much of the audience for popular plays. Identification with the devil is evoked to indicate ferocity as a positive as well as a renegade force as in the demonic identities of the 'rude boy' rock steady era. The 'rudie' culture was a precursor to the dance hall and as it was for the Guyanese popular theatre, the cinema was a strong influence with its gun-toting role models. Out of socio-political pressures which caused almost any form of rebelliousness and disobedience to be celebrated and violence to be a common metaphor came deviant creativity such as the 'fire pon rapid' speech rhythms of the dance hall DJ's in which verbal delivery and percussion patterns are designed to imitate machine gun fire, and shots are blasted off to show appreciation of a musical performance.

In many ways we are confronting a sensibility which is able to turn adversity into creativity[15] and whose fascination with the devil provoked a newspaper to comment in 1898 that in carnival 'to dress as the Devil seems to be most people's ambition.'[16] But even a contemporary calypsonian found it appropriate to use the mask of the devil as a metaphor to comment on evil and corruption in the society as he refers to the presence and guise of the devil everywhere: 'Yu fraid de devil / Yu fraid he bad / Well look de devil right in yu yard' (Penguin, 'The Devil'). The prevalence of demonic masks in the traditional theatre, the use of exhibitions of sexuality as weapon, and deviance as resistance to oppressive class and social pressures now find themselves rehearsed in contemporary popular theatre. The rehearsals of history continue as well, in middle class condemnation of this theatre. Gloudon (1982) reflects the views of a large portion of the middle class audience.

The Guyanese popular plays lack strength in the accomplishment of craft. This allows those who feel threatened because of the invasion by the populace of once exclusive domains to claim that their denunciation is a rejection of bad art.

But the middle class retreat from the popular stage is again a rehearsal of the withdrawal of the plantocracy from carnival when the ex-slaves joined in it after emancipation. However, the debate about appropriate methods of assessment of some varieties of Caribbean artistic expression revisited by Rohlehr (1989:10) refers. Rohlehr quarrels with Walcott's assertion that while the new radical poets writing out of the oral tradition are relevant and conscious of an audience, they 'leave out the most exciting part of poetry, which is its craft.'[17] He argues that 'what the oral tradition demanded . . . was an alternative notion of crafting, one that Walcott needed to resist because it ran counter to the models he had studied.'[10] Likewise, Brown and McDonald (1992) recognize the contentiousness of 'notions of form, craft and style' and that 'the cassette and the DJ are becoming as central to the dissemination and discussion of poetry as the literary magazine and the critic.'[18] The new forms of popular plays exert pressure on the conventional text because of their particular way of relating to an audience and the fact that their communication with that audience is effective. The performance text seems appropriate in its own arena. Nevertheless, while the Guyanese popular plays challenge conservative critical yardsticks and certainly suspends moral judgement, they have created no new dramatic form; the plays are by no means experimental, generally sticking to the conventional.

The element of sensationalism is high because of the graphic reflection in these works of folk and street culture as they exist, flavoured by popular myths or 'old wives tales' and crassly presented in defiance of conservative middle class sensitivities. Sexual intrigue at street level is often linked to the casting of diabolic spells since the audience believe that women seek to entrap men with the assistance of obeah and various prescribed charms. The comic value of this practise holds premium on stage because men who fall unsuspecting victims of it, usually seen as emasculated, are ridiculed by society. They are then put forward as the butt of derision on stage. The various other confrontations of domestic life including illicit love affairs added to the fact as it appears, that the ills of the society have greater audience appeal than its virtues, make these popular plays potentially excellent material for examinations of social struggle or human relationships including gender issues. Because it often exhibits life at grassroots level and communicates so well with a large audience who often participate vocally with remarks or expressions of approval or disapproval of the behaviour of the characters, this theatre has the power of moral influence.

Bascom, who once boasted in an interview[19] that during the performance of his plays, the car park is almost empty but the house is sold out, seem satisfied that his audience is from the less affluent sectors of society. He, as well as the less accomplished Vivian Williams exhibit an interest in moral issues with which this audience can identify. Bascom in particular, often makes his characters cause tragedy because of their sins, their folly or even indiscretions in a theatre of

44

sometimes bleak determinism. His better works may demonstrate the value of the popular play. This may be seen as well even in some of the other playwrights, but to a great extent, they do very little with their material beyond voyeuristic laughter. Yet, even that cannot be dismissed as totally useless.

Hollingsworth and Danns achieve at least a confrontation of some social issues avoided as indelicate in other theatres, which they exploit for humour. This may be cathartic, but their interest is commercial and generally because of the use made of the popular theatre by the dramatists, it is itself a demon. In an ironic way it continues the cycle of Satanic rehearsals because it invites the people into the theatre to confront the devil, not to exorcise him from their midsts or to equip them with the necessary consciousness to eliminate him from society, but to laugh acquiescently at his machinations. In several instances the playwrights fail to represent vice, immorality or folly in such a way that any moral statement is made. At times they rather seem to encourage or celebrate the baser aspects of unacceptable behaviour; or their technique is sufficiently faulty to leave the matter innocent of any direction.

Beyond mild shocks in the language, the sexuality and the frankness of some presentations, there is little rebellion or resistance but much amorality, and the audience is not frequently moved to a better state of being or understanding for having seen the plays. The revolt against middle class drama having been won, few further gains are made as most of the playwrights have been unable to maximize the opportunity beyond the creation of income from the theatre. Ironically, the Guyanese inheritors of popular theatre of resistance do not, like reggae singer Max Romeo ("I'm gonna put on a iron shirt / and chase Satan out of earth") attack the forces that oppress them, but rather condone and profit from the presence of the devil in society. Penguin's words continue: 'If you praise / The wrongs men do / Well then yu is / A devil too.' But the popular dramatists mirror the society and Rohlehr (1989) sums it up appropriately. "Society is diabolic because it has permitted the devil to exist.'

---

1   Gilkes's *Couvade* (1974) was the major Guyanese drama in Carifesta, Georgetown, 1972. A revised version (1990) was produced by Gilkes in Guyana (1993).

2   *Sweet Talk* (written c.1972) is Abbensettes's best known play and the only one known and performed in Guyana. But he has written many others performed in London and elsewhere including his latest, *The Lion* (1993). He reports that his work, which includes BBC Television series *Empire Road*, has been studied at two American Universities where he was Writer in Residence.

3   Pilgrim's (1926-1989) *Miriamy* (1963) written in 1955 and first performed 1962, is perhaps the most successful Guyanese comedy. Although he also published *Skeleton at the Party: a play in one act* (1954) and has written a

number of other dramas, most of the current theatre-goers and practitioners in Guyana believe that *Miriamy* is his only play.

4   Abdur Rahman Slade Hopkinson (1934-1993) is well known for his involvement in theatre on the UWI campus in Jamaica in the 1950's, with Derek Walcott's Trinidad Theatre Workshop and with the University of Guyana in the 1960's. His major works include poetry, and plays *The Onliest Fisherman*, published by UWI Extra Mural, and *A Spawning of Eels*, directed by Dennis Scott at the Barn Theatre in Kingston under its new title *Sala* (1974).

5   Norman Eustace Cameron (1903-1983) was a very prolific author whose plays were important in the mid twentieth century. Although they have great value in the history of Guyanese drama, their style and concerns would hold little interest for today's Guyanese audience..

6   Bascom 1986.

7   Gilkes's winning entry, *A Pleasant Career*, on 'the life and times of Edgar Mittelholzer', was written earlier and, before the Guyana Prize, won the Theatre Company Playwriting Competition in Georgetown, 1991.

8   [Georgetown slang] An arranged marriage for immigraiton purposes.

9   [Georgetown slang] A predatory female, often slick, attractive, who knows her way around the rough street life. Trades on her good looks for survival.

10   Gloudon 1982: 63-69.

11   Also a radio serial in the late 1970's, aired in Trinidad and Guyana. The stage *Beulah* plays.

12   See Cooper 1993, also Cooper's article 'Flirting with Pornography' in *The Village Voice*, New York, November 1992.

13   in *Just- / spring / when the world is mud- / luscious the little lame / balloonman whistles far and wee . . .* Cumming's untitled poem is referred to as "Chanson Innocence" [song of innocence].

14   Gordon Rohlehr 1992: 24-25. See also Warner-Lewis 1991.

15   Rohlehr 1971 (Sept-Dec): 92-113.

16   *Port-of-Spain Gazette*, Feb.14, 1898. Quoted by Errol Hill 1972.

17   1989 'The Shape of that Hurt', Introduction to *Voiceprint*. London: Longman. Also published in Rohlehr 1993.

18   Brown and McDonald 1992.

19   Interview with Desiree Wintz, Sunday Magazine editor, in the *Stabroek News*, Georgetown, Guyana.

Orature, Politics and the Writer:
A Case Study of Ngugi wa Thiong'o's Novels

Kabir Ahmed

Introduction

Any consideration of Ngugi wa Thiong'o's novels would indicate that he is primarily a politically-oriented writer. His novels reflect on political developments in Kenya, from the 1890's, when Europeans first set foot in East Africa, to the contemporary period, when the local elite have assumed positions of leadership. The later novels foreground Ngugi's ideological commitment and constitute an urgent call for the uprooting of neo-colonial capitalism and its replacement with socialism.

Reading his novels chronologically, it is clear that Ngugi passed through various phases of ideological development: from cultural nationalism to political nationalism and then to his maturation as a radical Marxist , with an unmistakable bias for the oppressed members of his community.

This paper sets out to examine Ngugi's adaptation of the devices of the oral tradition in his novels.[1] Contrary to an assertion that only *Devil on the Cross* (1982) utilises the devices of orature,[2] I will argue that all Ngugi's novels employ them in varying degrees. They appear in a small measure in *The River Between* (1965), an early novel; they also surface in *Petals of Blood* (1977) in appreciable quantity. They also appear in *A Grain of Wheat* (1967), the focus of a useful study on orature in Ngugi's fiction.[3] The essay dwells essentially on the significance of speech or its absence and how Ngugi manipulates this important aspect of orature to convey his socio-political statement about post-independent Kenya.[4] Ngugi's use of orature, however, reached its apogee in *Devil on the Cross*, a story in which the Kenyan novelist, for the first time, determined to communicate with Kenya's peasantry.

Perhaps right from the beginning, Ngugi had, through his use of the oral tradition in fiction, unconsciously wanted to communicate with a non-literate audience. But it is obvious that communicating with a largely uneducated and illiterate audience through a novel is difficult. After Ngugi wrote *A Grain of Wheat* he expressed disenchantment with the novel and the English language, because as he had observed, if he hoped to bring about social change through his writing he was engaged in a fruitless exercise since his work could not reach the people about whom he wrote.[5] This was probably why Ngugi tried his hand at drama, (of which more later) a medium through which he could speak to a wider spectrum of his Kenyan audience, although even then language was a major impediment until he switched over to the use of Gikuyu as a means of literary expression. The more he wrote in English, with all the frustration this involved for him, the more aware he became of the need to delve into and master his rich Gikuyu cultural and linguistic heritage. At the same time, he became conscious of the need to find ways to represent that cultural world in fiction if he really hoped to communicate with his primary audience, the Kenyan workers and peasants.

Ngugi's keen awareness of the important role of literature as a tool for social change and political education led to his continuous search for appropriate forms and language of communicating with his primary audience. In *Decolonizing the mind* (1986) Ngugi announced his farewell to the English language and declared that in future he would write only in Gikuyu, the language in which *Devil on the Cross* was conceived and written. But even when written in an indigenous language the 'text' has limitations in a society such as Ngugi's, where the majority of the population is still illiterate. One aim of this paper is to examine the strategies Ngugi employs to overcome the problem of communicating with a largely illiterate audience via a novel.

However, it was with drama that Ngugi was initially more successful in putting his message about the necessity for socio-political change across to a wider spectrum of the Kenyan people. The Kenyan novelist fully shares Augusto Boal's view that "the theatre is a weapon. A very efficient weapon (used by the ruling classes) as a tool for domination...But the theatre can also be a weapon for liberation".[6] I will look briefly at Ngugi's use of references to the oral tradition in his dramatic work towards the conclusion of this paper.

I

As an early novel, *The River Between* understandably contains artistic flaws which Ngugi was able to avoid in his later work. Although the novel was meant primarily as an exercise in cultural nationalism in which Ngugi sets out to protect and promote the cultural integrity of Gikuyu people, it is arguable that Ngugi felt compelled to frown at the same cultural institutions he cherished, because at the time when he wrote his first novel his Christian faith was still intact. The young writer was thus being pulled in two directions, trying simultaneously to celebrate his allegiance to both interests.

The novel, as an exercise in cultural nationalism, is disappointing. That disappointment is partly due to Ngugi's scanty use of aspects of orature which would have enriched the cultural texture of the narrative and firmly placed it in a traditional milieu. Although Ngugi creates the picture of a traditional society that prides itself in the knowledge of tribal secrets and its cultural heritage, that picture fails to come to life due to the absence of, for example, any significant use of proverbs, a form in which traditional wisdom is often encapsulated. Chege, one of the characters in the novel, is a traditionalist, whose reference as "the true embodiment of the Gikuyu"[7] who "knew more than any other person, the ways of the land and the hidden things of the tribe" (p.7) fails to convince. Apart from his reference to the Gikuyu creation myth there is little in the novel to link him to the rich and highly variegated folkworld of the Gikuyu. In the same way, Ngugi's attempt to imbue Kabonyi's character with traditional aura fails. As a traditional figure Ngugi should have given him the kind of speech through which his knowledge of tradition can be transmitted. At one point in the novel, Ngugi comments that Kabonyi "could speak in proverbs and riddles, and nothing could appeal more to the elders, who still appreciated a subtle proverb and witty riddles". (p.95) But we have to take this statement on trust as this aspect of traditional culture is rarely used.

When proverbs are used in the novel - as in connection with Waikayi, whose fame we understand "grew from ridge up to ridge and spread like fire in dry bush." (p.105) such usage of orature is often clumsy and amateurish. Ngugi was yet to demonstrate any real grasp of the cultural depth and variety of Gikuyu folkways. Knowledge of orature has to be acquired. Its employment in fiction has to be cultivated. Being an African does not automatically confer one with the knowledge and ability to use orature. In this regard, I share Eileen Julien's argument that:

> ....there is nothing more essentially African about orality nor more essentially oral about Africans. (But) to say this is not to question an African predilection for words well expressed...What must be recognised, it seems to me, is that speech/listening is a mode of language as is writing/reading. The art of speaking is highly developed and esteemed in Africa for the very material reasons that voice has been and continues to be the more available medium of expression, that people spend a great deal of time with one another, talking, debating, entertaining. For these very reasons, there is also respect for speech and for writing as communicative and powerful social acts.[8]

Because of all this, therefore,

> Neither (orality nor writing) should serve as metonymies for African or for European. Speech and writing are modes of language, and both modes are ours when we have the means to produce them.[9]

When Ngugi came to write *Petals of Blood* his grasp of orature was deeper, and his employment of it in the novel more confident. In the novel, set in Kenya, twelve years after independence, Ngugi combined the resources of his oral cultural heritage with modernist fictional techniques to convey his disgust at the collusion of the local elite with international monopoly capitalism in activities seemingly designed to dispossess the Kenyan peasants and workers.

This new confidence is underscored in Ngugi's attempt to articulate his message through selected aspects of the oral tradition in *Petals of Blood*. He uses several songs in the novel, from the very light-hearted ones to those which carry muted political messages. With reference to the circumcision ceremony Ngugi uses *Mumboro*, a traditional Gikuyu song, to make a point about Munira, one of the central characters in the novel. *Mumboro* is usually performed four months before initiation. It is very hectic and requires machismo and agility because: "the dancing takes the form of a contest between teams of boys from different villages....it may include a shoulder pushing contest" during which participants "sometimes hurt themselves seriously and cowards run away."[10] Ngugi tells us in *Petals of Blood* that

> Munira liked the dances: but it always made him sad that he
> could not take part, that he did not really know the words, and
> his body was so stiff. So he only watched, feeling slightly left
> out, an outsider at the gate of somebody else's house.[11]

Munira's inability to participate in the songs and dances is used to underscore an important aspect of his personality: he is a cultural assimilé whose exposure to Western education and values has cut him off from his tradition. His alienation from his cultural tradition also serves to reinforce his stance towards the fate of neo-colonial Kenya. He is an outsider in the attempt by others, such as Karega, to be part of the "force that would change things and create the basis of a new order" (p.294).

Munira has a moralistic vision of Kenya's solution to its neo-colonial predicament. Accordingly, he acknowledges the imperative to "change people's hearts" (p. 306) and create "a new world" (p. 295) of Christian brotherhood in which 'misguided' characters such as Karega should be rehabilitated from "thinking that he and his workers could change this world" (p. 299) and 'depraved' ones like Wanja be subjected to 'death by fire'. However, Ngugi's materialist vision in *Petals of Blood* prevents him from developing Munira's option, indeed it is shown to be a dead end, rather he endorses Karega's radical alternative means of changing the community.

Another *Mumboro* song in which Njuguna and Nyakinyua participated, putting on a dramatised rendering of it, can be likened to a musical opera, complete with a chorus. Towards the end of the performance, the uncommitted

Munira joins in and interrupts its steady flow thereby inviting chastisement from Nyakinyua:

> You now break harmony of voices
> You now break harmony of voices
> It's the way you'll surely break our harmony
> When the time of initiation comes. (p. 209)

Nyakinyua then throws a challenge in song, "If a thread was broken, to whom were the pieces thrown to mend them into a new thread?" (p. 209).

Abdulla, a veteran Mau Mau activist, responds by saying:

> When the old thread was broken, it was time, it was time for the whole people to change to another tune altogether, and spin a new and stronger thread. (p. 209).

In the context of the novel, the song indicates that the nation is no longer under colonialism. It is now under neo-colonial capitalism. Such a new, subtler, form of colonial subjugation calls for a change of strategy. Old solutions, such as traditional sacrifice suggested by Mwathi wa Mugo, an oracle, when Ilmorog was facing a drought, must be revised. It was decisively replaced with a vigorous and more radical solution - the trek - proffered by Karega. This is in line with Ngugi's refusal in all his later novels to romanticise traditional society, arguing that although much can be learnt from traditional institutions and customs, the African past must be viewed critically with the priorities of an emerging socialist society in mind.

Through the medium of *Gitiro*, a Gikuyu wedding song[12], which has been adapted in *Petals of Blood*, Nyakinyua comments on Ilmorog's recent history, describing how the people had been turned into paupers and asks "who had swallowed all the wealth of the land?" (p. 210). She then puts the drought afflicting Ilmorog into a wider historical and legendary context. She sings of struggles, starting with those which had occurred during the colonial period before focusing on the present ones and exhorting the youth:

> "to drive out foreigners and enemies lodged among the people: it was always the duty of youth to fight all the *Marimus*, all the two-mouthed Ogres, and that was the meaning of the blood shed at circumcision." (p.210)

Incidents involving story-telling are also used in *Petals of Blood* as a device familiar to his intended readers who would be comfortable with the cultural contexts which bear on such occasions. In the attempt to carry out Karega's suggestion of a trek to Nairobi by an Ilmorog delegation, Abdulla, one of the main characters exhibited his talent for story-telling, alerting the reader to his link with the oral culture of the Gikuyu. The journey to Nairobi is a journey of knowledge which Ntongela Masilela accurately observes, "maps a historical awareness of the Ilmorog community to the evils of capitalism and neo-colonialism."[13] Earlier on, Abdulla had narrated, to the delight of the younger members of the delegation, the tale of 'Ant and Louse', 'How Chamelon defeated Hare in a race' and 'How and Why Moon became enemies'. Later when the Ilmorog delegation meet their Member of Parliament, Nderi wa Riera, and it comes to Abdulla's turn to speak he communicates through the parable of the Hare and the Antelope. Both animals fell into a hole. Hare asked the Antelope to let him out by climbing on his back. After that he will help him out, he promised. After emerging from the hole, the Hare dusts himself and starts to walk away leaving the Antelope inside the hole. Says the Hare:

> The trouble with you, Mr. Antelope, is that you go jump-jumping leap-leaping in the air instead of firmly walking on the ground and looking to see where you are going. I am sorry but you have only yourself to blame. (p.179).

The above parable is a clear indictment of the political elite, who, after riding on the back of the common people to power, now ignore them leaving the to wallow in despair, in the teeming problems they - the elite - had promised to eliminate.

In *Petals of Blood*, such problems are actually compounded by the political and business elite who have not only dispossessed the powerless members of the community but have also, at each turn, frustrated their attempts to lead a decent existence in modern Kenya. For example, Abdulla is a representative small businessman emasculated by the system. A Mau Mau veteran, his only 'reward' in independent Kenya is a small shop, and when he is later bought out of his brewery business by "the new black landlords" (p.326) be becomes an orange seller. Another victim, Wanja, who is sexually exploited by Hawkins Kimeria, is conceived in terms of a blighted flower with "no stigma or pistils... inside... A moth-eaten flower (which has been) prevented from reaching light" (pp 21-22). As a result of her exposure to the harsh realities of capitalist Kenya, she is kept from the light and is therefore denied the opportunity of living the life of a decent citizen. Notwithstanding Ngugi's use of orature in *Petals of Blood*, the message of such a novel could not reach the people about whom it was written. It is a novel written in English and largely depending, as I observed earlier, on modernist narrative techniques.

II

It was when Ngugi was in prison in 1978 that it occurred to him to write *Caitaani Mutharaba-Ini* (1981) later on translated into English as *Devil on the Cross* (1982). Having successfully written and staged *Ngaahika Ndeenda* (1980) (translated as *I Will Marry When I Want*) (1982), the play which led to his imprisonment, Ngugi had suddenly realised that through the vernacular he could reach and perhaps communicate with the majority of his intended audience.

The issue of communication with peasants and workers had been troubling Ngugi for a very long time, since he wrote his first major political novel, *A Grain of Wheat* in fact. After completing his third novel at Leeds in 1966, Ngugi had, as I mention above, publicly voiced his disappointment that the peasantry whose lives and concerns fed the novel could not read and understand it.[14]

However, with *Devil on the Cross*, which - in addition to being written in Gikuyu - generously employs aspects of the Gikuyu oral tradition, Ngugi's intention is to reach the Kenyan peasants and workers, the sector which he feels duty-bound to mobilise into revolutionary action, comes closer to being fulfilled. One might argue that although by writing in the vernacular Ngugi aims to reach all Kenya's dispossessed, in reality, he can only reach those Kenyans who understand Gikuyu, just one out of more than forty linguistic groups existing in Kenya. But the wide circulation of Ngugi's message among the Kenyan peasants and workers would not be adversely affected since *Devil on the Cross* had since been translated into Kiswahili, a language widely spoken and understood in Kenya. Neither would the potency of his message conveyed in Gikuyu orature be diminished, given the affinities existing in the motifs of African folktales from different linguistic groups.[15] Thus, the employment of elements of Gikuyu orature combined with the use of Gikuyu language to make *Devil on the Cross* a story that can appeal to illiterate peasants and workers when it is read to them in "market places, bars, outside factories during lunch breaks, and around the fire at home in the evenings", in a country which has a strong story-telling tradition.[16] This practice helped Ngugi to overcome the problem of how an illiterate audience can have access to a written text.

Ngugi has employed many aspects of Gikuyu orature in the novel but because of the limited scope of this paper, I can consider only a few of them here.[17]

One of the most important techniques of orature adapted by Ngugi in *Devil on the Cross* so as to sustain the attention of his audience is that of story-telling. Early in the story, Ngugi writes that:

> Certain people in Ilmorog, our Ilmorog, told me that this story
> was too disgraceful, too shameful, that it should be concealed
> in the depths of everlasting darkness. There were others who

claimed that it should be suppressed so that we should not
shed tears a second time. I ask them: How can we cover up
pits in our courtyard with leaves or grass, saying to ourselves
that because our eyes cannot see the holes, our children can
prance about the yard as they like?[18]

The conversational style of that excerpt is characteristic of most of *Devil on
the Cross*, which is essentially cast in the mode of an oral tale. The semblance of
story-telling is further created by the narrator's use of direct address to the
listeners, such as "Let me tell you the lesson Wariinga taught that man" (p.221)
and towards the end of the story the narrator tells his listeners, "You who were
there, what more can I say?" (p.246).

To emphasise the oral quality of *Devil on the Cross*, Ngugi uses the variant of
a *gicaandi* player to narrate the story. According to C. Cagnolo, in Gikuyu society,
a *gicaandi* player is a professional raconteur who "goes round the country like a
medieval storyteller (stopping at) markets and squares to sing his poem to the
accompaniment of his bottle-gourd."[19] His offering "may go on for a whole day"[20] for
the benefit of an audience whose interest in the material would normally glue them
to their seats listening to a story they might already have heard but would enjoy
hearing over and again depending on the skill of the raconteur. Adopting this
character and adapting his narrative technique, would, in Ngugi's view, ensure that
the attention of his audience is sustained.

The main reason why Ngugi is determined to capture the attention of his
audience is so as to convey the message that the Kenyan middle-class elite is
exploitative and therefore deserve condemnation from the Kenyan masses. The
elite in the story are presented in such a way as to invite the wrath of the masses,
both by their physical appearance and then through their pronouncements.

Ngugi uses pointed and carefully selected local images to describe some
members of the middle-class elite. One of his intentions is to hammer home the
point that neo-colonial capitalism has dehumanised its champions beyond
redemption. One of them, Gitutu,

had a belly that protruded so far that it would have touched
the ground had it not been supported by the braces that held
up his trousers. It seemed as if his belly had absorbed all his
limbs and all the organs of his body. Gitutu had no neck - at
least, his neck was not visible. His arms and legs were short
stumps. His head had shrunk to the size of a fist. (p. 99).

Similarly, the mouth of Gitutu's companion, Kimeendeeri wa Kinyuanjii,

is shaped like the beak of the red-billed ox-pecker, the tick
bird. His cheeks are as smooth as a newborn baby's. His legs
are huge and shapeless, like giant banana stems or the legs of
someone who is suffering from elephantiasis ...
His neck is formed from rolls of fat, like the skin of the hairy
maggot. (p. 186).

Both figures have lost the use of their human faculties and they typify the
Kenyan middle-class elite, seen in the story as a dependent and parasitic class,
who live entirely on the sweat of the peasants and workers. Their high drive for
women and food, dwelled upon in the story, corresponds with their insatiable
appetite for the material benefits they derive from economic exploitation. Since the
exploitation is seen in terms of "drinking of blood of workers....milking of their
sweat (and) devouring of their brains" (p.187) it is not a surprise that the Kenyan
bourgeoisie should also be portrayed as "a class of man-eaters" (p.186) who inflict
physical and emotional wounds on the weak with impunity. For the creation of his
ogre-like characters, Ngugi drew heavily on the Gikuyu oral tradition, which is
rich with stories in which "ogres known as *Marimo* in the vernacular"[21] feature
prominently. In *Agikuyu Folktales* (1966) Ngumbu Njururi records several tales
about "the one-legged, two-mouthed cannibalistic ogres of East African tales."[22]
One of them, "Konkeyi and His father the Ogre"[23] is horrific as it involves the
slaughtering and eating of a human victim that Konkeyi and his father caught.
When they finish their feast on the woman, who had been pregnant, Konkeyi
collects the three babies he found in her womb, takes them to his mother and asks
her to cook them for him. His mother, a human being, married to Konkeyi's father
against her wish, cooks three mice for her son instead and secretly brings up the
three babies. The babies belonged to her sister who had been on her way back
home when Konkeyi spotted her on a tree and joined his father in killing her. The
three babies grow up into men and later kill Konkeyi and his father, thus giving
the woman who had saved them the freedom she needs to escape. In *Devil on the
Cross* the Kenyan masses are asked to compare the middle-class elite with the
"one-eyed ogres" (p.37) in Gikuyu folktales who can attack and insensitively
devour human beings alive. Once the comparison is made it would then be easy for
Ngugi's audience to understand that, at least in the author's view, the
extermination of human beings who are as callous as ogres is not only justified but
is also their primary duty as Kenyan citizens.

Another instance in the novel when such grotesque figures are drawn by
Ngugi in order to invoke the wrath of his audience is during the competition in the
Cave before the International Organisation of Thieves and Robbers. Here the
monstrous representatives of the Kenyan elite reveal their strategies for further
emasculating the peasants and workers by the total monopoly of air, water and

land. They are all seeking, via the debate, to win an 'exploitation trophy', but in reality they are making confessional statements which, since they are about exploitation and repression in neo-colonial Kenya, will certainly enrage Ngugi's audience.

During the debate, Ngugi invites the audience to laugh at the figures who employ self-praise as a means of winning the coveted trophy of exploitation in this world of overturned values. One of the characters who resorts to self-praise is Kihaahu wa Gatheeca, who delves into the storehouse of Gikuyu orature, likening himself to "the cock that crows in the morning (silencing) all the others."

He further tells the gathering that:

> I am the lion that roars in the forest, making elephants urinate.
> I am the eagle that flies in the sky, forcing hawks to seek
> refuge in their nests. I am the wind that stills all breezes. I am
> the lightning that dazzles all light. I am the thunder that
> silences all noise. I am the sun in the heavens during the day.
> I am the moon, king of the stars at night. I am the king of
> kings of modern theft and robbery. (p. 109).

Some members of Ngugi's audience who are familiar with the rich world of Gikuyu proverbs will know that the author has an ironic intention in asking the figures to recommend themselves before the Visiting Robbers. This is because a Gikuyu proverb, one of several recorded by C. Cagnolo in the *Akikuyu: Their Customs, Traditions and Folklore* reads "self praise is no recommendation,"[24] a translation of the original *Kanyoti Kabariti Keminagera njoya*.

Ngugi would certainly concur with Ruth Finnegan's assertion that "songs can be used to report and comment on affairs for political pressure, for propaganda, and to reflect and mould public opinion."[25] Although song is put to maximum use in *Devil on the Cross*, it is actually in drama that Ngugi exploits it fully as a potent instrument of articulating his revolutionary message. His Gikuyu play, *I Will Marry When I Want*, was first staged in Kamiriithu in 1977 and was banned after only a few performances. The play was proscribed after the Kenyan authorities realised that Ngugi was using the dramatic medium to re-tell Kenya's history from the perspective of peasants and workers. Ngugi was also aware that the sense of identification of the audience with the performance would be strong if recognisably local songs were used in a play. The author therefore used in his play traditional songs such as the *Gitiiro*, which his audience might know because it is the classic song performed at Gikuyu wedding ceremonies.[26] It was then easy for Ngugi to use traditional tunes to fit in the revolutionary exhortations carried in the several songs in *I Will Marry When I Want*. The songs carry explicit protest messages meant to stimulate the latent Gikuyu revolutionary awareness as the two examples below illustrate:

> We do not mind being jailed
> We do not mind being exiled
> For we shall never stop
> Agitating for and demanding back our lands
> For Kenya is an African people's country.[27]

and

> The Trumpet of the masses has been blown
> Let's preach to all our friends.
> The trumpet of the masses has been blown
> We change to new songs
> For the revolution is near.[28]

The banning of the play by the Kenyan authorities in December 1977 and the official order stopping the rehearsals of *Maitu Njungira, Mother Sing For Me*, (1981) a dramatic musical evoking the response of Kenyan workers against the labour conditions of the 1920s and 1930s, show that oral forms can be used in drama to directly communicate with the masses; and in the hands of a left-wing writer like Ngugi they can prove dangerous to a repressive regime as they can be collectively marshalled to serve as an instrument of public incitement.

Mother Sing For Me was first performed in 1982 and because of its popular appeal, it was banned soon afterwards as we saw. But by the time it was proscribed already twelve to fifteen thousand people had seen it.[29] The musical uses songs from certain Kenyan ethnic groups such as Gikuyu, Luhya, Kamba and Luo. Like the songs contained in *I Will Marry When I Want*, those in *Mother Sing For Me* emphasise communal solidarity and aim to awaken the revolutionary awareness of the people. One of the songs runs thus:

> Unity! Unity!
> Of us workers and peasants
> And our fearless courage
> Are what will liberate Kenya!
> Are what will liberate Kenya.[30]

Given the effect of *I Will Marry When I Want* and *Mother Sing For Me* it is arguable that drama is more suited to an illiterate audience such as Ngugi's. It is also true though that, given the story-telling tradition in Kenya, Ngugi's *Devil on the Cross* has been a successful experiment which blends the vernacular with aspects of orature and really has been able to reach the ordinary people for whom it was written.

---

1   Discussion in this paper is limited to *The River Between* (1965), *Petals of Blood* (1977) and *Devil on the Cross* (1982). Limitation of scope became necessary so that detailed examination of orature in the above novels could be carried out. The novels excluded, such as *Weep Not, Child* (1964) and *A Grain of Wheat* (1967), belonging, for the purposes of this study, to the first phase, utilise aspects of the oral tradition in small quantities. But *Matigari* (1987), Ngugi's recent story, written in Gikuyu, is a fable set in contemporary Kenya, about a hero who takes his name from the title and is embroiled in a search for 'truth' and 'justice'. It thus belongs to the later phase, sharing a common bracket with *Devil on the Cross*.

2   See Julien 1992: 42, where she states that "...his reference to that tradition is more recent..."

3   The essay, referred to in the next note, was kindly brought to my attention by Dr. Stewart Brown, the convenor of the C.W.A.S. round-table Conference and editor of the proceedings.

4   Jackson, 1991.

5   "I felt I dealt with Kenyan or African institutions so intimately. Then I felt that people who fed the novel, that is the peasantry, as it were, will not be in a position to read it. And this was very painful. So I really didn't see the point of writing anything at all". See Reinhard Sander and Ian Munro, 1984: 48.

6   Boal, 1979:ix.

7   Thiong'o' 1965: 44. The present and subsequent references will be to the 1983 edition, reset in 1975 with page numbers immediately following the cited passages.

8   Julien, 1992: 24.

9   Ibid.

10 Sicherman 1990: 221.

11 Thiong'o 1977: 207. The present and subsequent references will be to the 1978 edition with page numbers immediately following the cited passages.

12 Rosemarie Muthoni Morton, Personal Interview, 8th April, 1988.

13 Masilela 1979: 20-21.

14 Sander Reinhard and Ian Munro, 1984: 148.

15 For example *Marimu*, Gikuyu term for ogre is *dodo* in Hausa (a Nigerian language) and *debul* in Krio (a Sierra Leonean language). Also the Yoruba have *Abiku* a child who falls sick and dies and comes back to the world, through its parents. The Hausa equivalent of that is *Danwabi*.

16 Bjorkman, 1989: 3.

17 For a more detailed examination of aspects of orature (such as proverbs, songs, parables and etc.) in the story see my "Oral Tradition as an Instrument for

Revolutionary Change in Ngugi wa Thiong'o's *Devil on the Cross*" in *Ufahamu* Vol. XX, No. 1, 1993.

18 Thiong'o', 1982: 7. The present and subsequent references will be to the cited edition with page numbers immediately following the cited passages.

19 Cagnolo, 1933: 166.

20 Ibid.

21 Cagnolo, 1952-53 p. 64.

22 Finnegan 1970: 355.

23 Njururi 1966: 11-13.

24 Cagnolo 1933: 216.

25 Finnegan, 1970: 272.

26 Cagnolo 1933: 171.

27 Thiong'o' 1982: 26.

28 Thiong'o' 1982: 115.

29 Bjorkman 1989: 60.

30 Quoted in Bjorkman 1989: 75.

A Tale of Two States: Language, Lit/orature and the Two Jamaicas

Carolyn Cooper and Hubert Devonish

The norm which is accepted in the international community is that a state should ideally be made up of a single national/ethnic group speaking a single language. Such notions have their origins in the Europe of the late Middle Ages, following the break up of the Holy Roman Empire. This ideal of what a state should be has spread across the world in the wake of European expansion and domination. The ideal has been universally accepted in spite of the fact that the states which appeared in Europe hardly ever fitted the model.

For a state to survive, those over whom control is exercised have to generally accept the legitimacy of that state. People, therefore, have to be presented with a body of ideological justifications for the existence of the state and its authority. One such justification is that the state is the highest expression of a shared national identity. The claim that this identity exists is based on cultural characteristics which are considered to be common to members of the group but not to others. Where a common national identity does not exist, it is usually suggested that such an identity is in the process of being forged. Another justification is that within the state there exists a common language which permits communication between all citizens of the state. Where such a common language manifestly does not exist, the governing groups propose that it is emerging and/or being spread as part of the process of nation building. National identity and language identity become linked when, as often happens, one of the cultural features a national group claims to share is a common language.

The notion of a language is itself a cultural construct. Speakers of a series of related language varieties may, at a particular point in their history, come to view these speech forms as belonging to a single entity, a language. These speakers begin to perceive this shared language both as a medium of communication among themselves and as a means of distinguishing members of their own group from members of other groups.

Several factors may trigger the change in language consciousness which gives rise to the notion that a language exists. One such factor is the appearance of written language. Speech has its disadvantages. Up until the 20th century, it could not be used to communicate without the potential audience being within earshot as the speaker produces the message. Writing is a form of technology for representing language which gets around these difficulties. The reader does not need to be present at the time and place where the writer produced the message. A written language message has as a potential audience anyone who can gain access to the surface on which the written symbols have been marked. In reality, of course, such access is restricted. Only two options exist. One could physically transport one's self to where the written message is located. Otherwise, potential readers could have the written language message physically transported to them.

Printing solves the dilemma of restricted access to single written bodies of language messages. It created the possibility of multiple copies of the same language message. Access was not now limited to the original form of the message. The existence of multiple copies multiplied several times over the size of the potential audience for any written message.

With all its obvious advantages, writing, particularly when enhanced by the application of printing technology, came to be perceived by speakers as the primary form of language. It was a short step from this to the conclusion that only those forms of speech which can and do appear in writing and print, are true languages. In societies possessing writing, nearly all use of the prestige language in public formal situations has its origins in writing. Public speeches, lectures, news broadcasts, etc. are mainly produced by speakers reading scripts aloud to an audience. In diglossic situations, therefore, the primary function of diglossia for that section of the population which controls the 'High' language is to preserve a monopoly over both the prestige language and writing itself.

Literature is produced when language is used creatively in the written medium. Purely oral forms of verbal creativity, for example proverb, folk tale and popular song, that have their origins in the language of the 'Low' culture tend to be devalued in the conservative, monopolist discourse of literates. The combination of creativity and written language produces strong feelings of emotional identification in many speech communities. Literature creates a focus for the language consciousness of members of the speech community. It provides them with an ideal image of what the language is or ought to be. In diglossic situations, language consciousness becomes focused around the 'High' language used in public formal, written and literary contexts. 'Low' language varieties, spoken in private and informal situations, have no recognition as constituting a language in and of themselves. The reasoning which gives rise to this perception is that such varieties have no writing system and, therefore, no literature. Consequently, they do not constitute a language. At best, when recognised as being different from the 'High' language, they are regarded as broken forms of that language or of some other language which possesses writing and literature.

The Jamaica Case

In Jamaica, diglossia is a long established feature of the language situation. There is a cluster of language varieties which occupy the position of 'High' language in the diglossia. These are varieties which members of the speech community identify as English. In popular consciousness, these varieties have the characteristic that they are 'a language'. English has all of the features which a language is supposed to possess. Among these is a standard and well known writing system and a solid body of literature. The English literary tradition dates back to Chaucer, Shakespeare, Milton and the King James Version of the Bible.

The position as the 'Low' language in the diglossia is occupied by language varieties which members of the speech community would describe as 'patwa', 'dialect', 'bad English' etc. These are varieties which linguists often grace with the term 'Jamaican Creole'. For purposes of this paper, we will use this term interchangeably with 'Jamaican'. These varieties traditionally do not appear in the writing of native speakers. They consequently have no literature.

In their "Introduction" to *Voices in Exile: Jamaican Texts of the 18th and 19th Centuries*, Jean D'Costa and Barbara Lalla confirm that as early as 1740 "connected discourses" in Jamaican appear in print. The early recorders of Jamaican were, most often, expatriate British writers who were fascinated with native life and wished to document its curiosities as accurately as possible. One such curiosity was African-derived polygamy. Robert Charles Dallas' *The History of the Maroons* (1803) records a conversation between a Jamaican Maroon and a proselytising Christian, attempting to convert the Maroon from polygamy:

> "Top, Massa Governor," said he, "top lilly bit - you
> say me mus forsake my wife." - "Only one of them."
> - "Which dat one? Jesus Christ say so? Gar a'mighty say
> so? No, no, massa:Gar a'mighty good: he no tell somebody
> he mus forsake him wife and children. Somebody no
> wicked for forsake him wife! No, massa, dis here talk no
> do for we."[1]

Dallas, recognising Jamaican as a distinct language, offers an English translation:

> In other language thus: 'Stay, Sir', said the Maroon, 'stay a
> little. You tell me that I must forsake my wife.' - 'Only one
> of them.' - "And which shall that be? Does Jesus Christ
> say so? Does God say so? No, no Sir; God is good, and
> allows no ʋᵔᵉ to forsake his wife and children. He who
> forsakes his wife must be a wicked man. This is doctrine,
> Sir, not suited to us.'[2]

Given the intention in all these cases to record and document actual speech which had been heard, there is some question as to whether most of these could qualify as literature, i.e. creative written language in Jamaican Creole.

There does exist in these Jamaican Creole language varieties, however, an established body of creative oral language. But Jamaica is a society which requires that varieties possess writing before they gain a place in public consciousness as constituting a language. Jamaican Creole varieties, therefore, fail the language test. They cannot be recognised as constituting a language in their own right. The most liberal traditional position assigned to them, as a result of the similarity in their vocabulary with English, is that of a dialect of English. The English language proper is perceived as being made up of those varieties which have writing and an established literature.

In Jamaica, there is a long tradition of creative writing in European languages, mostly in English and some Latin. The extraordinary Franciscus Williams is the 18th century precursor of succeeding generations of literate Jamaicans who defined their humanity in terms of their ability to master "learned speech". Williams, to whom Edward Long devotes a chapter in his multi-volume *History of Jamaica* is a classic example of this early type. According to Long, Williams,

> being a boy of unusual lively parts, was pitched upon to be
> the subject of an experiment, which it is said, the Duke of
> Montagu was curious to make, in order to discover,
> whether by proper cultivation, and a regular course of
> tuition at school and the university, a Negroe might be
> found as capable of literature as a white person.[3]

In his Latin "Ode" to George Haldane, Esq., short-lived Governor of Jamaica (the English translation is Edward Long's), Williams anticipates the preoccupations of later elitist-nationalist Jamaican poets writing in European languages. He may live in the tropics, not England, and his body, like that of his black Muse, may be "clad in sable vest," but he is nevertheless culturally "white" because of his eloquent control of European language and literature. Linking colour, race, national identity, language and letters, Williams assimilates into Western culture. He thus proves himself worthy of self-government in pre-emancipation Jamaica:

> We live, alas! where the bright god of day
> Full from the zenith whirls his torrid ray:
> Beneath the rage of his consuming fires,
> All fancy melts, all eloquence expires.
> Yet may you deign accept this humble song,

Tho' wrapt in gloom, and from a falt'ring tongue;
Tho' dark the stream on which the tribute flows,
Not from the skin, but from the heart it rose.
To all of human kind benignant heaven
(Since nought forbids) one common soul has given.
This rule was 'stablish'd by th'Eternal Mind;
Nor virtue's self, nor prudence are confin'd
To colour; none imbues the honest heart;
To science non belongs, and none to art.
Oh! Muse, of blackest tint, why shrinks thy breast,
Why fears t'approach the Caesar of the West!
Dispel thy doubts, with confidence ascend
The regal dome, and hail him for thy friend:
Nor blush, altho' in garb funereal drest,
Thy body's white, tho' clad in sable vest.
Manners unsullied, and the radiant glow
Of genius, burning with desire to know;
And learned speech, with modest accent worn,
Shall best the sooty African adorn.
An heart with wisdom fraught, a patriot flame,
A love of virtue; these shall lift his name
Conspicuous far, beyond his kindred race,
Distinguished from them by the foremost place.[4]

The work of the prolific, early twentieth-century novelist Herbert DeLisser, must be noted, particularly since he authored *Jane's Career*, the first Jamaican novel in which the central character is a native speaker of Jamaican Creole. That novel, published in 1914 marks another stage in the representation of Jamaican Creole in written texts. Bilingual native Jamaicans are beginning to represent in their own written texts the reported speech of native speakers of Jamaican. Somewhat like the early non-native recorders of eighteenth and nineteenth century Jamaican Creole speech, DeLisser faithfully documents Jane's speech as a kind of curiosity - local colour.

By the 1930s, there was an intensification of effort in Jamaica to contribute to the body of literature already existing in English. The material was inspired by life in Jamaica and the Caribbean and language varieties in use in Jamaica. The bulk of this material was in those varieties identified as English by the community. This literature was coming from the small minority who, like the eighteenth-century Franciscus Williams, had both literary skills and a high level of competence in these English varieties. The *Focus* literary magazine which was published in 1943, 1948, 1956 and 1960 and which was first edited by Edna Manley, the English sculptor and painter who was married to Norman Washington Manley, founder of the People's National Party, reflected an insurgent Jamaican nationalism.

This literary production was the result of significant changes in the consciousness of the Jamaican educated elite. They were beginning to see themselves as having a distinct identity and set of interests from the ruling British colonial elite. As an expression of this consciousness, they were producing literature in local varieties of English. These were language varieties they themselves used and with which they were identified. There was another aspect of this literary production. The vast majority of the population were speakers of varieties of Jamaican Creole. These people had little or no control of English. The literature produced, therefore, also served to mark off the educated elite from the mass of the population.

The literary output in local varieties of English marked the emergence of a sense of national identity centred around the educated elite. The monolingual Creole speaking population was peripheral to this consciousness. According to elite perception, the mass of the population would have to be brought out of the dark into the light. With enlightened government, they would be taught literacy and acquire competence in English. The educated elite, aided by this new sense of national identity, were able to lead a movement which culminated in the achievement of self government and, eventually, political independence. The state thus created was based on a sense of national identity shared by a tiny elite to the exclusion of the vast majority of the population.

There were some limited efforts on the part of literates in English to produce literature exclusively in the varieties of Jamaican Creole. The work of Louise Bennett in particular stands out. She wrote down traditional Jamaican Creole Anansi stories. In addition, she produced a large body of original writing, mainly poetry, in the language. Several of her poems satirise the elitist nationalist movement for independence. For example, "Independance" (the pun on dance mocks the "song and dance" of the occasion) wittily contrasts the ordinary Jamaican's sense of self-importance with the Government's newly acquired status as independent nation. Bennett emphasises the disparity between official conceptions of the nation state and the everyday, small-scale politics of individual empowerment:

> Independance is we nature
> Born an bred in all we do,
> An she glad fe se dat Govament
> Tun independant to. (*Jamaica Labrish* 169)

There were two difficulties facing Bennett in her attempts to write in Jamaican. Her readership was made up of literates like herself. Anyone who had acquired literacy had done so in English. There was no perception within any sector of the population that a linguistic system other than English existed in Jamaica. For example, the distinguished Jamaican man of letters, Rex Nettleford, in his 1966 introduction to Bennett's *Jamaica Labrish*, describes Jamaican Creole as "an idiom whose limitations as a bastard tongue are all too evident." (Bennett, 1966, p.10)

Bennett's struggle, in the first instance, was to achieve 'dialect' status for this bastard tongue as is expressed in her poem 'Bans o' Killing'. (Bennett, 1966, pp. 218-210). The argument was that English-speaking communities in Britain had regional dialects. The fact that Jamaica also had a regional dialect should be recognised without embarrassment. She, therefore, had to employ the notoriously inconsistent conventions of the English writing system to represent a language which had a sound system quite distinct from that of English. Given her ideas at the time about language, she adopted the conventions of English non-standard dialect writing, replete with apostrophes and alterations to normal spelling not justified by any pronunciation difference. Her decision to write Jamaican and her choice of writing system achieved her immediate objective of giving Jamaican Creole 'dialect' status amongst the literate English-speaking elite.

The later Louise Bennett, moving beyond the conception of Jamaican as a dialect of English, herself contests the popular "corruption of language" view of Jamaican. In "Jamaica Language" which she performs on her album Yes M'Dear - Miss Lou Live (Island Records ICT9740, 1983) Bennett argues humorously that English is just as "corrupt" as Jamaican since it is derived in part from Norman French, Greek and Latin. Jamaican should be recognised as similarly "derived" from other languages. Having tested the limitations of the corrupt bastard-language, Jamaican, Bennett has succeeded in helping to legitimise it. Part of the legitimising process has been the writing down of the language. Bennett, herself, insists that she is a writer: "From the beginning, nobody ever recognised me as a writer. 'Well, she is 'doing' dialect'; it wasn't even writing you know. Up to now a lot of people don't even think I write."[5]

But the choice of an inappropriate writing system had an important additional effect. Many persons who were literate in English and also spoke Jamaican Creole could claim with some justification that Jamaican Creole material was difficult to read. Such claims emphasised the superiority of the standard 'language', English, relative to its non-standard 'dialect', Jamaican Creole.

The production of Jamaican Creole material in an English writing system had another difficulty. The only people who could read it were, of course, the literates. However, all of these had acquired their reading and writing skills in English. Thus, even the Creole material that Louise Bennett was writing was ending up with largely the same readership as that written in Jamaican varieties of English. The work by Bennett and other similar writers could not initially, therefore, become the focal point of a language consciousness among the majority of non-literate speakers of Jamaican in the population.

The way Louise Bennett in particular tried to get around this problem was by doing public performances of her work. From the point of view of trying to create a Jamaican Creole language consciousness, however, there was an enormous difficulty. The very fact that this material was reaching a mass audience in an oral form and not in writing only served to confirm existing popular attitudes. Even illiterates shared the view that the special category of 'a language' was reserved for language varieties which could be shown to be widely written.

An important potential solution to the writing system dilemma became available in 1961 with the publication of *Jamaica Talk* (Cassidy 1961, p. 433). Like the lay-person, Bennett, the linguist Cassidy, to some degree, represented Jamaican as a 'dialect' of English. In the appendix to *Jamaica Talk* Cassidy presented a consistent, phonemically based writing system for Jamaican Creole, which was further discussed and illustrated in the introduction to the *Dictionary of Jamaican English* (Cassidy & LePage, 1980, pp. xxxvii-lxiv). It had the important advantage of not employing any symbols not used in the orthography of English.

In spite of Cassidy's concession to the English writing system, the vast majority of educated literates saw no reason over the years to go to the trouble of learning a new writing system for a set of language varieties which were not 'a language' proper. Mervyn Morris, editor of Louise Bennett's *Selected Poems* gives the common-sense rationale for the writer's choice of an English-looking orthography for Jamaican:

> But, anxious not to be rejected unread most of us
> have chosen compromise. The most common (if
> inconsistent) approach is to write the vernacular
> for the eye accustomed to standard English, but
> with various alterations signalling creole.[6]

Over time, however, with the strengthening of a mass based nationalism, alternative views have appeared. For many members of the society, the very difference in the sound values assigned to letters in the Cassidy system makes Jamaican 'look' on the page like a language totally distinct from English. For some, this is a deterrent. However, for those wishing to assert the autonomy of a Jamaican national identity, the non-English look of the written language is an advantage. The very strangeness of the orthography restores to Jamaican its integrity; it gives the language and its speakers presence. The 'writability' of Jamaican in a coherent, discrete system thus confirms its status as 'a language', just like English.

For example, Mr. Andrew Sewell, a Jamaican Creole speaking Rastafarian man, having read a newspaper article written in the Cassidy system, "Cho! Missa

Cargill, Riispek Juu!" (Cooper 1989) goes straight to the heart of the matter: "It ful di spies af owa riel Afrikan langgwij:" "It fills the space of our real African language". The Cassidy orthography, making manifest the languagehood of Jamaican Creole, seems to fill the void left by African languages which have all but disappeared from everyday use in Jamaica. This more positive approach to the Cassidy writing system has been relatively recent, however.

In circumstances of considerable resistance to the general use of an efficient writing system for Jamaican, between the 1960s and the present, a small but growing body of Jamaican Creole literature, mainly poetry, has been emerging. A popular sense of national feeling, not to be confused with the elitist kind on which the Jamaican state is based, has been developing quite rapidly among the mass of the population. The speed with which the sense of this alternative national identity has been spreading has quickly outstripped the limited expansion of literature written in Jamaican Creole varieties which has taken place. Here was a developing popular sense of national identity crying out for a means of expression in a truly popular body of creative language.

Twentieth century technology came to the rescue, providing a way around the writing problem. Technologies involving sound amplification, tape recorders, gramophone records and radio had made it possible for spoken language to reach much larger audiences than was possible in face-to-face interaction. These technologies did for the spoken word what the printing press had done for writing, i.e. multiplied several times over the potential size of the audience for any particular language message. Language transmitted using these technologies, as happened with earlier technologies such as writing and the printing press, came to acquire special status. It is by this means that, with the emergence of radio in Britain, BBC English could come to have at least partly replaced the English of Milton, Shakespeare and the Bible as the model for standard varieties of British English.

Initially, the new technologies were used to expand the communication network of the elite groups within Jamaica. Soon, however, the elite monopoly of these technologies began to collapse. Radio drama programmes and more recently television serials in Jamaican, as well as popular radio talk shows that give widespread voice to speakers of Jamaican Creole - some bilingual programme hosts even speak in Jamaican - have been an important mechanism for developing a truly populist national consciousness.

In addition, in the 1960s, there developed popular local music forms in ska, rock steady and reggae. These forms were promoted and popularised through sound amplification, gramophone records and radio. In the early period, the lyrics of this music were predominantly in language varieties which would be regarded as English or a close approximation thereof. The chorus would often be in some variety of Jamaican. Examples of this kind of song range from 'The Israelites' by

Desmond Dekker, through 'Maccabee Version' by Max Romeo to 'No Woman No Cry' by Bob Marley. There was an alternative trend involving songs with predominantly Jamaican Creole lyrics, such as 'Sweet and Dandy' by The Maytals and 'Ramgoat Liver' by Pluto Shervington. Some of the songs of this era were used in the movie *The Harder They Come*, which itself became a 'cult' film, replete with English sub-titles for foreign audiences unfamiliar with Jamaican, defining for non-Jamaicans, as well as Jamaicans, the essence of a subversively anti-establishment Jamaican national identity.

It should be noted that most of this early music was first produced in the recording studio from lyrics which were either improvised or already written. The music reached a mass audience, primarily through gramophone records being played with amplification at dances and in other public places, as well as over the radio, It is usually after gaining popularity through these media that the music would be performed by singers and bands before a live audience.

With the appearance of systems of sound amplification which allowed both the recorded music and the disc jockey presenting it to be heard at the same time, the practice developed at dances by the beginning of the 1970s for disc jockeys to do live talking improvisations against the background of recorded music. To facilitate this, the recording studios began to produce reverse sides of 45 rpm records with only the bass and rhythm tracks of the music. Against this musical background, deejays as they came to be called, would deliver improvised lyrics to live audiences. These lyrics were predominantly in varieties which would be described as Jamaican Creole. Over time, a new genre developed, known variously as dub, rockers, deejay and dancehall. After multiple presentations in the dance hall to live audiences, particular deejay pieces get recorded and reach a wider audience through cassette tapes, gramophone records, compact discs, the radio and most recently music videos on television. This deejay art form has produced over the years many well known performers, e.g. U-Roy, Yellow Man and the relative newcomer Shabba Ranks, who won the 1992 U.S. Grammy award for Reggae music.

The fact that the background music is often identical for several deejay pieces suggests that what is central here is the lyrics. The music is simply a medium for conveying the language form and message created by the deejay. The audiences in the dance hall provide instant feedback, with the deejay, where necessary, adjusting the lyrics in line with the public response. In general, the process of creating and refining a deejay piece is entirely oral, with the only fixing of the form taking place when it is eventually recorded.

Writing plays little role in the traditional deejay performance mode. In an interview, Lovindeer, a performer of deejay music who often takes off the lyrics of other deejays, reports that unlike most performers, he resorts to writing in the process of creating a piece. He keeps a note book of ideas to which he refers when he begins to compose. He explains that the fact that he does not produce his work in live dance hall situations allows him the option of not working in the predominantly oral mode of the mainstream deejays. But there are some deejays who do claim to write their lyrics, for example, Lecturer - as his sobriquet would suggest:

> Dadi Lekcha wan di lirikal tong/Daddy Lecturer, the
>   one with the lyrical tongue
> An diijie kom, an mi naa go ron/And if a deejay comes,
>   I'm not going to run
> Pon di groun mi sit doun/On the ground I sit down
> Wid mi pen an mi piepa/With my pen and my paper
> Mi rait mi liriks doun/I write my lyrics down
> An mi stodi it, an ina dans haal/And I study it, and in
>   dancehall
> Mi fling it doun/I fling it down

The deejay phenomenon has helped create an environment in which the production of literature in Jamaican Creole can flourish. A body of poetry has developed which is written to be performed to the same kind of musical accompaniment as that used by deejays. Several dub poets as they have come to be known, have attracted public attention and a significant body of dub poetry has emerged. Some of the outstanding poet performers are Linton Kwesi Johnson, Oku Onuora, Jean Breeze, Mikey Smith and Mutabaruka. Oku Onuora defines 'dub poetry' in such a way as to suggest its distance from the conventions of English metrics. It may be written down, but he disclaims any genealogical ties with mainstream English literature:

> It's dubbing out the little penta-metre and the
> little highfalutin business and dubbing in the
> rootsical, yard, basic rhythm that I-an-I know.
> Using the language, using the body. It also
> mean to dub out the isms and the schisms and
> to dub consciousness into the people-dem head.
> That's dub poetry.[7]

It is the historian and poet Edward Kamau Brathwaite, who in his book *History of the Voice*, makes the most precise connection between language and national identity in his coinage of the term "nation language" to define indigenous Caribbean languages such as Jamaican Creole. He argues, somewhat metaphorically like Onuora, that "[w]hat English has given us [as] a model for poetry, and to a lesser extent prose (but poetry is the basic tool here), is the pentameter.... There have, of course, been attempts to break it."[8] He continues: "It is nation language in the Caribbean that, in fact, largely ignores the pentameter."[9] 'Dub poetry' thus marks an important stage in the development of non-elitist nationalist consciousness in Jamaican Creole, among Jamaicans at home and, equally importantly, in communities of migrants the world over. However, this material is nowhere as popular, nor as much a part of mass consciousness as is mainstream deejay music.

The deejays have produced a significant body of creative language in varieties of Jamaican Creole.[10] For example, the British based deejay, Macka B, at the December 28, 1991 "Best of White River Reggae Bash" concert in Ocho Rios, recognised the achievements of world-famous Jamaicans who "big-up" the nation:

> Nou yu si Jamieka/Now you see Jamaica
> Jamieka iz so fiemas all uova di worl/Jamaica is so famous all
>   over the world
> Jamieka hav so moch dan an danet iz anbiliivabl/ Jamaica
>   has so many "war-lords" and "war-Queens" it's
>   unbelievable.
> Aal uova di worl dem rispek Jamiekanz, siin?/All over the
>   world they respect Jamaicans, seen? (Agreed?)
> So hier dis nou! A *capella*!/ So hear this now! A *capella*!
> Fi soch a smaal ailan/For such a small island
> In di Kyaribiiyan/In the Caribbean
> Yu projuus huol hiip a dan man an wuman/You produce a
>   whole heap of men and women
> In Jamieka, ina Jamieka,/In Jamaica, in Jamaica
> Lisn mi nou!/Listen to me now!
> We yu get dem fram, Jamieka?/Where do you get them from,
>   Jamaica?
> We yu get dem fram?/Where do you get them from?
> Yu mosi mek dem in a fakchri/It must be that you make them
>   in a factory
> Pan di ailan (rep.)/On the island (rep.)
> Marcus Garvey, im woz a griet man/Marcus Garvey, he was a
>   great man
> Baan ina Jamieka, ina Sint An/Born in Jamaica in St. Ann
> Tek Blak kanshasnes to di Amerikan/Took Black
>   consciousness to the Americans
> Shuo blak piipl wich paat im kom fram/Showed black people
>   where he came from

Bob Marley im waz a neks wan/Bob Marley, he was another
one
Tek rege myuuzik go a evri neishan/Took reggae music to
every nation
Im big-op Jamieka, big-op Rastaman/He enlargened
Jamaica, elevated Rastafari

Deejay music has reached a mass audience in Jamaica and other parts of the Caribbean. In addition, it has spread to Jamaica and other Caribbean communities in North America and Europe and expanded into significant sections of the non-Caribbean populations in these countries. It has developed a sizeable audience in countries around the world, as far away as The Ivory Coast, Israel and Japan. The international recognition being given to this material is acting as a substitute for the validation which would normally come from such material being written down and thus becoming literature. The effect is that the rapidly developing popular national consciousness in Jamaica is moving in the direction of acquiring a language consciousness to go with it. The notion of Jamaican Creole as a language separate and apart from all others is being fostered by international interest in the body of creative material produced in the language.

Additional support for this emerging language consciousness is coming from the status and prestige being accorded messages in the electronic media. Radio, television and the video may be replacing the printed work as the most prestigious medium for transmitting information in language. If this is so, this use of Jamaican Creole in these media can only further enhance the developing prestige of the language. The language has latched itself on to those communication media which are growing in importance. The effect of not having a standard writing system, and hence, a developed body of literature, is being minimised.

There is considerable historical precedent for what is happening in the Jamaican situation. States have emerged before as a result of national consciousness triggered by the appearance of an oral rather than written body of creative material in a language. The oral epics of the *Iliad* and the *Odyssey*, attributed to Homer, formed the bridge between the collapse of the Mycenean Greek state and the reconstitution of a Greek state system some 500 years later. These oral epics, performed to musical accompaniment in a tradition which seems rather similar to deejay music, formed the basis of preserving the Greek language and national identity over the centuries when no state existed. These epics were a major focal point of national identity when the Greek state was reconstituted. The oral epic has served similar functions among groups as diverse as the Malinke and Songhay of West Africa, and among the Serbs and Croats of Yugoslavia.

The Incipient Alternative State

The developing alternative national identity that has its early origins in maroonage and the traditions of slave resistance is paralleled by complementary developments at other levels of the society. At the level of the economy, there is the development of international trade involving itinerant traders known as higglers or ICIs (Informal Commercial Importers).

Other economic activities include the cultivation and export of marijuana as well as the transhipment of cocaine, all defined as illegal by the existing state structure. There is, as well, the assertion of a mass based alternative morality as expressed in what the establishment perceives to be the 'slack' or vulgar lyrics of much deejay music. Another aspect of this alternative morality is the glorification of gun violence, particularly that employed by gunmen against the forces of law and order, as evidenced for example in the movie *The Harder Thy Come*. This celebration of violence is reminiscent of the 'heroic' phase which many societies appear to go through in the process of developing state systems (Renfrew, 1987, p.182).

The heroic songs of the Serbs and Croats, the Vedic hymns of Ancient India, and the Greek *Iliad* are all works of oral art in which there is glorification of violence in pursuit of the national interest. These works serve to justify and legitimate the violence exercised by a national group on others in attempting to achieve its goal of creating a state within secure boundaries. This, of course, is normally only achieved by military action over all rivals.

An incipient alternative Jamaican state based on an alternative national identity and national language may be challenging the existing state structure. Since its rival is an existing state within the same physical boundaries, the struggle between the two takes the form of a conflict between the legal and the illegal, between competing moral codes, and at the level of language in a contest between English and Jamaican, between a 'High' versus a 'Low' language in a diglossia, and thus, ultimately between a literature and an orature.

---

1   Quoted in D'Costa and Lalla, eds. 1989: 18.
2   Ibid., 132.
3   Long, 1774; rpt. 1970, Vol. II: 476.
4   Quoted in D'Costa and Lalla, eds. 1989: 10-11.
5   "Bennett on Bennett", Louise Bennett interviewed by Dennis Scott, 1968.
6   Morris 1990 : 22.
7   Statement made at a seminar on "Dub Poetry", Jamaica School of Drama, January 17, 1986. Transcript of excerpts done by Mervyn Morris.
8   Brathwaite 1984: 9.
9   Ibid., 13.

10 See, for example, Carolyn Cooper, "Slackness Hiding From Culture: Erotic Play in the Dancehall" *Jamaica Journal* 22.4 (1989) : 12-20; 23.1 (1990) : 44-51 in which detailed analysis of more than 50 deejay songs is given. At the 1989 meeting of the Society for Caribbean Studies in Britain where I presented a version of this study, John Figueroa, editor of *Caribbean Voices* Vols. I & II suggested that I publish the lyrics of the deejays in the sample. But given the limited readership of written texts in comparison to the wide audience for electronic recordings, this seems to me a retrograde step.

Text, Tradition, Technology: Crossover and Caribbean Popular Culture

Curwen Best

Popular Caribbean art has for a long time and in a lot of cases existed at the margins of 'serious' critical comment and academic scholarship. This is so for a number of reasons. First critics have in many instances been out of touch with the actual goings on within contemporary popular culture. Many criticisms have held fast to the notion of the scribal as sacrosanct: a practice further reinforced by the New Criticism and its influence on many of the region's thinkers. From the political standpoint, the 'establishment' has overlooked popular poetics, which it finds too disruptive of the status quo.

But it should also be stated that the popular forms with which this paper deals, do themselves exert a kind of pressure on the critic. Since such forms as Kaiso/Calypso and the Folk song are performance and music centred, and call attention to linguistic and non/para linguistic elements, and to technological advances, they can pose particular problems to the approaches, tools, scope, concepts and language of scriptocentrists and literary traditionalists. Ruth Finnegan has highlighted this fact. She poses the question of 'how can these wider facets be recorded and represented and treated seriously as "real" formulations?'. And she goes on to provide part of the answer. For her there is a need to:

> move away from the older view of text as
> hard edged ... fully comprised by its <u>verbal</u>
> components, existing independent of its
> performance, analysable separately from other
> texts or other media....[1]

This paper therefore concerns itself firstly with foregrounding some of the components which comprise certain 'popular' forms. Thereby, and secondly, it sets up the framework within which the performer is <u>expected</u> to practice the craft. It goes on to explore how some artists respond to these 'textual' limitations and how they <u>re-shape</u> notions of the (fixed) text within their genre. Finally, it examines what is the ongoing relationship between the demands of 'tradition', and the everyday creative 'crossover' practices.

There are few texts which can tell the tales of the islands of the Caribbean in the way that the folk song does. The African Barbadian folk song "King Ja Ja" is one relevant example in this regard. It is with this song that the wider concept of 'text' which I want to present and explore can more aptly be demonstrated. "King Ja Ja" is a folk song which derives from the visit of Ja Ja, the king of the West African state of Opobo. (This region was an Igbo trading centre at the time of British commercial and military operations in the Gold Coast area around the late nineteenth century). When Ja Ja fell out of favour with the British, reputedly because of the 'competition' which he gave them, he was put on a ship and 'packed off' to the Caribbean.[2] It was during his brief three months stay there that the following song was created in Barbados:

> If you want to live in sin
> get a lil' house an put me in
> but if you start to play the fool
> ah'll get a big stick an' ah'll keep yuh cool

chorus:

> King Ja Ja won' leh Bekka 'lone
> King Ja Ja won' leh Bekka 'lone
> King Ja Ja won' leh Bekka 'lone
> Wha' Bekka got um is all she own

> If yuh love me treat me nice
> an' I will cook yuh peas an' rice
> But if yuh start to play the fool
> Ah'll get a big stick an' ah keep yuh cool[3]

As is the case with other such popular folk forms, its lyrics are but a part of the work. A fuller appreciation of its make-up is only experienced when music is added:

KING JA JA

It requires the singing voice(s), an acoustic guitar, congas, and little more in terms of musical accompaniment. When the drama surrounding Bekka and her suitor are played/performed, that is when the 'full text' is approximated. There should be a chorus of singers comprising male and female voices. And there has got to be the two protagonists. The chorus surrounds them in a semicircular arrangement and sings its own section following the male female flirtations of every verse. The two players command more of the spotlight. She wears an apron over her longish dress and carries a bucket balanced majestically on her head, in traditional Barbadian manner. He is regally dressed in colourful prints. This is a poem of statement and counter statement. It is an ongoing drama of materialistic and sexual expectation.

As components of Caribbean literature such genres as the folk song exhibit their own sense of 'text'. These popular forms are most effective when the lyrics, the tune, its musical accompaniment, costume, setting, dramatisation, and audience participation all come together to constitute (what can be called) 'the text in total'.

Over the years the processes and routines described above have quite consistently been retained in many performances. So that it is possible to speak of a master type text. However, there have also been performances which tamper with and embellish such master type texts. Some performers (especially musical accompanists) have brought their own personal musical influences to bear on scores like the one set out above. There are often differing melodies. One common melodic interpretation tends to render the 'A' natural crotchet in bars one and three of the chorus as 'F' natural; and there are numerous other melodic variations. There are musicians who (presumably to create a more effective sense of movement around the third and fourth beats in bars one and three of the chorus), who treat the 'F' major chord prescribed above, as something closer to the 'F' suspended chord. The antepenultimate and penultimate bars are also occasionally coloured with much more intricate chord progressions than the one offered above.

Although I am not arguing that such popular arts have a hard edged text, I want to make the point that any performance which is seen as veering too sharply away from the kind of presentation (of "Ja Ja") outlined above, does open itself to possible audience (Bajan) disapproval: anything between lukewarm audience interaction and applause, or a cold indifference. These are the kinds of tensions inherent within the practice of some performance centred Caribbean art forms. Much of this tension centres around question/notions of tradition, creativity, and intertextuality.

Kaiso is a form of Caribbean oral/sung/music poetry which can arguably be considered as a variation and continuation of the folk song tradition. Unlike the previous genre though, kaiso centres more so on the single performer than on a choral unit of voices.

A common reaction by kaiso traditionalists to its ongoing series of progressions has been one of scepticism. Some have overtly resisted kaiso's dynamics, and others have attempted to impose fixed rules on the genre. Among this latter group of prescriptivists are some artists, cultural political administrators, and indeed certain audiences. The now legendary kaisonian Roaring Lion is insistent (for example) that what is sung by most singers as 'calypso' is not really what constitutes 'the calypso'. For him a kaiso must be built on eight lines to the verse and four lines to the chorus.[5] For him therefore, kaiso's structure is fixed and hinges on a particular stanzaic form. This becomes its text. Others like Lord Executor have been less dogmatic. Although Executor had expressed his reservations about the movement from the minor to the major mode, he became more accepting of kaiso's transformations in his later practice.

The suggestion of there being a master text in kaiso, is perhaps best born out in the procedures surrounding kaiso competitions in the Caribbean. In contemporary practice there is a lot of prestige associated with winning these competitions. But to be kaiso queen or king the performer must find 'the right formula'. From a field comprising scores of singers s/he must go through a series of eliminations before possibly reaching the finals. At 'finals night', each kaisonian performs at least two original songs (composed and rehearsed beforehand), within a given time frame, and in the presence of vibrant and vocal audiences who in some cases exceed fifteen thousand. The judges usually number about eight. Although the emphasis in allocating points might vary from island to island, performers are judged within the categories of melody, lyrics, rendition, originality, and presentation. This represents the order of descending importance, with the most points being awarded for melody and lyrics, and the least for originality and presentation. Judges are on occasion challenged to make clear and public, what constitutes 'the formula'. Sometimes judges do take up the challenge, but they often become embroiled in an unending debate.

In the more recent history of kaiso competitions the 'winning formula' has tended to privilege lyrics of social and political redress, and a musical composition built around a slow, or a slow-to-medium tempo rhythm ($\textit{d}$ 80-90). The determination to fulfil the criteria set out for the competition has created many a rift between fellow artists, and in some cases a sense of alienation between some artists and the art form. Some singers have officially withdrawn from public practice because of the art form's rigid demands.

Arguably, the most radical response this century by the kaiso performer against institutionalised notions of a master text in calypso, came about in the 1970's. The emergence of Soca as an extension (a co text) of the kaiso art form symbolised a movement towards freer practice. It would supposedly allow the artist the freedom to create without the restrictions of calypso proper. Soca became less concerned with 'hard hitting' commentary, and even less interested in the standards of assessment by which kaiso is judged. So that artists like Arrow from Montserrat stood at the forefront of innovations within this neo-kaiso movement. Such performers were pioneering 'crossover' musical developments, and utilising such features as repetition of words and music to create aesthetically pleasing, rhythmically exciting 'up tempo' and catchy compositions.

In Barbados however, some performers were responding to the pressures of the kaiso art form in a slightly different way. They were drawing simultaneously from the musical developments in soca and from traditional kaiso's didacticism. This movement was not exclusive to Barbados, but arguably, it was in Barbados that these advances were being most consistently pursued.

The kaisonian Gabby is one such performer at the forefront of the calypso genre. He has been operating from within the genre, but he has simultaneously been challenging its boundaries. Together with the Guyanese producer Eddy Grant, they have been exploring the resources of the kaiso art form, and redefining its text. It is important to see how Gabby epitomises the kaiso tradition, yet how his practice challenges the genre's sense of a fixed text.

His songs encompass the major areas of the 'classical' kaiso tradition. He has composed socio-political,[6] nationalistic,[7] humorous,[8] witty[9] and satirical songs,[10] songs of male female inter/counter-play[11] and songs which fall into the category of the 'kaiso war' ethos.[12] In addition he is a noted exponent of the traditional practice called 'picong', which is an improvised practice. As within traditional kaiso where the rhymed couplet and the use of nation language are basic components, these are also to be found in his work. His songs continue to be developed around a basic structure that progresses from band chorus, to verse, to chorus, and through the band chorus again. His images and symbols are predominantly rooted in the experiences of the society. Gabby continues to perform in both the formal setting, and at less formal occasions. He is equally effective whether performing with an eighteen piece brass band, or providing his own accompaniment on his twelve string acoustic, in the 'old time' fashion. He is very much dependent on his audiences to make his work 'complete', to interpret the signs inherent in his presentation and to interact within the procedures of each performance. This relationship is best exemplified in a composition like his 1983 song "Boots", an anti militarism song which was very popular in the Caribbean, and a song which caught the attention of Time magazine. Its antiphonal and call and response structures are noted strengths of the work. He utilises these most effectively in the live context.

> Is it necessary
> to have so much soldier in this small country?
> NOOO NO NO NOOOoo
> Is it necessary

to shine soldier boots wid tax payers' money?
NOOO NO NO NOOOoo

BOOTS BOOTS BOOTS an more BOOTS
on de feet of young trigger happy recruits
BOOTS BOOTS BOOTS an more BOOTS
marching threatening army troops[13]

His innovative tendencies are most evident in his musical experiments, in his mid 1980's experiment with a type of lyrical imagism, and in his most recent attempts to introduce the pop styled love ballad into the kaiso idiom. Although some of the musical experiments to which this essay refers, were produced as vinyl/plastic texts, they still do represent offerings for new ways of perceiving the art form.

The 1982 song "Jack" was the first in a consistent series of didactic kaisos in which he utilised an up-tempo soca rhythm. It also replaced the more conventional drum phrasing of the time with rhythmic inflections derived from his nation's own nineteenth century indigenous percussion band (Tuk band). His musical innovations would in subsequent years also inspire the wider use of pop phrasing in drum tracks. And these patterns were played not always by the 'live' drummer on acoustics, but at times by the Linn drum. Some ten years after his experiments with synthesised samples of live brass within his compositions, more and more artists have now adopted this practice instead of actually using 'live' horns. So that the days of 'live' brass being a compositional necessity for constituting the kaiso text are now slowly passing.

The female male interplay in a popular theme in the calypso art form. A substantial percentage of songs have unfortunately treated the female as an object of sexual gratification. The soca movement has itself also presented the 'woman as object' motif as integral to its text. What is textually innovative about some recent Gabby performances which treat of the female is their movement away from the soca formula of: man meets woman in a fete; man and woman 'jam' in the fete. His compositions have also been subverting kai/soca's musical text.

In a composition like "Melvina", the emphasis is not on a physical relationship. It centres on the agony of female male misunderstandings and on the state of human helplessness when love breaks down. Hence the persona persistently pleads, in vain, with his departing lover to 'come on come on come on come on come on back':

Don't you remember
always fought together
we know that we would
would never leave each other[14]

Similarly, in the song "Only Cheating"[15] the composer undermines the preconceptions loaded in his song's title, and presents a song in which two victims of broken relationships seek solace in each other's company. The act of cheating is not treated as a consequence of lascivious passion but is presented as being a more comfortable lifestyle than remaining with uncaring partners, and being beaten 'black and blue': 'if my woman got man, and your man got woman'.

One of his most recent experiments in this mode is "Guilty":

> If you see me girl when you walk down the street
> don't you walk on by on me
> say to me hello baby please say hello
> don't you walk on by on me (baby)

chorus:

> Guilty honey guilty baby
> I am guilty what can I do
> guilty honey guilty baby
> I am guilty of loving you
>
> If you see me call when you say not to call
> and you hang up on me
> and the phone it rings once again off the wall
> I'll be calling back baby (baby)[16]

Gabby the kaisonian subverts his musical text and comes up with a song which has elements of reggae 'lovers rock' up front in the mix. The down beat of the drum track carries a 1970's reggae groove but this is played against a stated kaiso strum on the guitar: maintaining a link between the artist and the tradition on which (most of) his work is based. He sings in the cosy voice of the 'pop' balladeer.

If such interactive discourses (as this one) highlight the limitless intertextual possibilities open to the artist, they also foreground the perils of defining what constitutes 'tradition' (in a pure sense) in some contemporary Caribbean popular art forms.

---

1   Finnegan 1992: 51.
2   Cookey 1974 and Martin 1983.
3   Marshall 1981: 12
4   Roaring Lion on Voice of Barbados' "Fireworks" 1992.
5   Marshall, Folk Songs 11.
6   For example the song "One Day Comin Soon" on the album *One In De Eye*, ICE BGI 1001 (1986).
7   The Gabby composition "Culture" (1985).

8   Gabby composition "Bow!Wow!Wow"c(1988).
9   Gabby "Mr.T" (1983).
10 Gabby's "Miss Barbados" on *One In De Eye*.
11 "Needles an Pins" Wirl SH 001 (1979).
12 "De List" on *One in De Eye* approximates this category.
13 Gabby's "Boots" on *One In De Eye*.
14 "Melvina" on *Across The Board* ICE BGI 1010 (1989).
15 "Only Cheating" on *Illegal Tender* BGI (1990).
16 "Guilty" on *Soca Trinity* (1993).

Making Space For Orality On Its Own Terms

Philip Nanton

Continuum theory has for some considerable time exercised a strong influence over analysts' efforts to incorporate the diverse Caribbean oral and written traditions within a single framework. With its notions of 'fluidity' and 'continuity', the theory has emphasised the interaction between written and oral art forms. The limited distinctions which it does make tend to focus on questions of technique. The argument of this essay is that such a focus ignores a number of features of orality which make it distinctive.

There are, in fact, two important features which distinguish orality. These are conceptual and circumstantial. At the conceptual level, historical analysis suggests that it is possible to trace an identifiable epistemology of orality and that this has been its driving force. Oral concepts are reflected in ways of structuring and composing ideas which are unique. These can occasionally be discerned in scribally dominated contemporary societies. In terms of the circumstantial differences between the two forms, the centrality of performance to orality gives it a number of distinctive characteristics associated with time; audience; and particular forms of word play and phrasing linked to locality.

Continuum theory and orality

The development of continuum theory is derived from reactions to the false boundaries imposed by colonial domination in the Anglophone Caribbean. Colonialism enforced the primacy of elite standard and text. These demands denied the legitimacy of orality in the prestigious centres of colonial society in each territory. Three such centres were the world of education, where the dominance of learned standard English was enforced by formal grammar training in schools, secondly, the application of official and standard English in the legal system and thirdly, in each of the centres of island government.

Throughout the century, the growing self awareness of the island countries in the region, reinforced by formal political independence, led to the incorporation of the diverse social and cultural resources many of which were denigrated and wasted under colonialism. The desire to incorporate, develop and exploit these differences in language and art forms was part of this impetus.

By 1970, the notion of a 'language continuum' could be taken for granted. For example, John Figueroa noted in his introduction to 'The Blue Horizons': "now that Derek Walcott and Evan Jones and Edward Brathwaite and Mervyn Morris among others, have used the West Indian language continuum creatively (and with a minimum of fear, hesitation, or self consciousness) our latent dreams will more and more be given unique form," (Figueroa, 1970, p.21).

Around this time the application of continuum theory to link oral and scribal art forms resulted in both linear and dialectical interpretations of the theory. In two seminal articles which utilise continuum theory and demonstrate its applicability to both society and literature, Gordon Rohlehr focused on the relationship between orality and text. In his analysis of 'Literature and the Folk' (1971), he argued that "a continuum exists between a living oral tradition and a growing scribal one in the West Indies. It relates to the continuum which exists between the various West Indian Creoles and Standard West Indian English. Most West Indians seem to enter this continuum at several points." He concluded that "most things in the West Indies are fluid, and most people caught in a series of interlocking continua, making it difficult to place anyone precisely..." (Rohlehr, 1992, pp. 115 and 121). Some twelve years later, he defined the relationship as "an aesthetic continuum stretching between forms derived from an oral paradigm, and forms suggested by various aspects of Modernist aesthetics." (Rohlehr, 1992, p.61). At one end of the continuum he identifies orality as concerned with 'energy, continuity and catharsis' expressed in religious and secular paradigms. At the other end, its counterpoint, modernity, is described as having as its focus the response to the void in various forms. He identified a number of significant artists of the region whose work either accommodates the continuum or is locked into a dialogue with one or other of its poles.

Others identify continuum theory as a linear notion. Kenneth Ramchand suggests that "the emergent levels of dialect can be ranged in a continuous scale between standard English and residual or hard-core creole." (Ramchand, 1971, p.90). Carolyn Cooper argues for an expansion of the continuum because its boundaries are too restrictive towards recent developments in Creole and these developments need to be incorporated into the mainstream. For example, in her analysis of the lyrics of Jamaican DJ's, she demands a redefinition of the rigid boundaries of the canon to accommodate the full Creole/English, oral/scribal range of verbal creativity (Cooper, 1989).

A number of anthologies indirectly reinforce the linear orthodoxy of continuum theory. Where distinctions between orality and text are drawn, their celebratory attitude to the material tends either to make light of boundaries or, when diversities are more fully explored, the diversity is interpreted as offering a variety of forms available for shaping. Paula Burnett's anthology *The Penguin Book of Caribbean Verse* illustrates this approach. In her introduction she concedes that the oral tradition contains "its own patterns of development and characteristic styles, distinct from those of the written tradition" (Burnett, 1986, p. xxviii). However, in her anthology boundaries between written and oral forms are identified as boundaries of convenience. She claims: "where there is an oral tradition alongside a written tradition with literacy the norm, distinctions become blurred and a good deal of cross-fertilisation from one tradition to the other occurs." For Burnett, the significant distinguishing feature between the two forms remains "the manner of transmission." (Burnett, 1986, p. xxviii).

Whichever approach the adherents to continuum theory adopt, their focus on the interaction between written and oral forms appears to reinforce a scribally dominated prosody. This diverts attention from the possibility of an alternative prosody based on such features as articulation, pitch, tone and tempo, which offer greater recognition to the specificities of orality. At least one critic has taken up this challenge, in a recent analysis of features of Caribbean orality, Best has identified the specific properties of orality through performance. He offers an alternative critique of orality by a focus on the musical properties inherent within work which is strongly influenced by orality. For example, in a review of Brathwaite's "The Arrivants", he conducts such an analysis, linking the proximity of voice to sound and hence to music. He argues, that there are certain performative, stylistic components, patterns, and traits which inform the make up of the poem 'Masks'. Based on his listening to the work in performance he concludes that "The Arrivants" is an orchestra of voices, with those compositions which feature Bajan voicings central to the performance success of the work. Best's critique however remains within a framework which for the most part accepts oral/scribal continuities. (Best, 1993, p.331).

The assumption of these continuities may be challenged in two ways. It is possible, firstly, to distinguish a distinct creative process, identified below as 'true' orality, which is different from those in scribally dominated societies, and secondly, to identify circumstances of performance suggested by three features, time, audience and forms of word play and phrasing associated with a locality, which lend a degree of specificity to orality.

1.   'True' orality

In Caribbean societies in which writing is the formal and politically dominant means of communication, it is useful to distinguish between 'true' orality and 'mock' or writer influenced orality. The latter is sufficiently powerful off the page to utilise the artifice of orality to good effect. Text is predominant because, to paraphrase Ong, dialogue is suspended till the reader comes along (Ong, 1990, p.206). In contrast, 'true' orality involves an epistemological break between the oral and scribal form in which a piece of work is created. There is both historical and contemporary evidence to demonstrate the distinctiveness of 'true' orality.

R.L. Enos has illustrated how, in ancient times, the diverse oral traditions of the sophists of the Mediterranean shaped the Attic-Ionic dialect which became the classical literary style of ancient Greece. Enos states: "during the classical period 'Greek' meant a diversity of dialects, each of which took shape by its features of oral discourse...Isolated by virtue of some of the most hilly terrain of the Mediterranean, multiple local dialects evolved throughout the Greek world... (in time) select features of dialects became incorporated into the dominant writing dialect... features of oral dialects that were considered effective and elegant were assimilated into the written style ...what was assimilated was not only words and phrases but also ...ways of structuring and composing ideas were transferred from the dialect into the grapholect." (Enos, 1990, p. 53 - 54)

At a general level, Greek/Caribbean parallels have in the past been noted, particularly by C.L.R. James. If the barriers of 'hilly terrain', which Enos describes, are replaced with the Caribbean Sea dividing its many islands, it is not difficult to identify through Enos' description of the isolation in which Greek dialect development took place similar scope for the diverse dialect development in the Caribbean. In the context of this scribal/oral debate, there are also two elements of Enos's argument which are worth reiterating. These are, firstly, that there are good historical grounds to support the idea that oral art forms can claim a legitimate space for distinct ways of structuring and composing ideas. Secondly, historical evidence suggests that orality places considerable importance on the specificity of words and phrases from a locality.

In the contemporary Caribbean, a sign of orality's distinct features has been conveyed in a discussion by Mervyn Morris about the uneasy relationship that exists between some performance poets and the translation of their work into print. After describing the artistry at work in the late Mickey Smith's creation of a performance poem; Morris notes, in contrast, Smith's 'unusual uncertainty' when it came to presenting his work on the page. In his collaboration with Smith for this purpose Morris noted: "His skills were essentially oral. When he showed me some of his poems in manuscript he clearly had little notion how he might effectively translate into this other medium the poems that had clearly worked in oral presentation." (Morris, op cit, p.9).

Here we have a statement of more than a problem of technique. The creative process which Morris observes is more than the skill of a meticulous artist. His description suggests how a clear break with the scribal form can be identified. Smith's approach appears to have been derived from a fundamentally different way of structuring and composing ideas for the voice.

Honor Ford Smith reinforces this observation in her description of the way in which Smith created a piece for performance, "he would work for hours and hours, sometimes the whole day, with his tape recorder which would have the backing tracks for the music, trying out different variations of rhythm. He was very conscious of the variety that he could get in his voice." (Morris, 1989, p.8).

2.   Circumstantial orality

Circumstantial orality arises out of the central relationship between orality and performance. Three aspects of this relationship can be identified. They concern audience, time, and aspects of word play. Each enable the analyst to draw certain boundary lines around 'true' orality.

Audience

The importance of shared norms as well as contact with the audience, both directly and as co-operative and co-determinative participants in discourse, are important to the oral tradition. Figueroa is one Caribbean anthologist who has recognised the significance of this relationship and its unique non-textual feature. In the introduction to "An Anthology of African and Caribbean Writing in English", he notes, in a discussion about the role of imagination in fiction: "judgements often have to be made about timing, about level of realism, about the reaction and sensibilities of the 'audience'. It is perhaps the ready availability of the last which differentiates the oral making of literature from the written." (Figueroa, 1982, p. x.)

In a rhetorical work, the sharing in the cultural norms between, for example, a storyteller or poet and his or her audience, is likely to be more important to orality than in text. The ancient art of memorisation most effectively brings these two together. Such a situation may occur in the modern world where, for example, a poet has only a rudimentary knowledge of writing.

It is commonplace for the sensitive actor to note that each audience is different. Similarly in storytelling, the craft is subject to the needs of specific occasions. The storyteller must constantly be aware of audience mood, altering expression, tone and temper to meet the situation created in the relationship with the audience. There is thus no scope for a 'fixed' text if this malleable art form is to hold the attention of the audience. Chukwuma offers a thumbnail sketch of the dynamism of this art form in the West African context identifying: "a miniature theatre where the audience sit in a semicircle facing the narrator who is protagonist (he/she) must not only be heard, but seen. It is a dramatic performance with gestures, voice modulations, facial twists, dramatic body movements like, jumping...elbow edging, rhythmic leg flexing...running, wrestling..." (Chukwuma, 1981, p. 13). The issue here is not that the written text is incapable of dynamism but the dynamism of orality.

Central to orality, then, is the active involvement of the audience. This can involve more than the nominal Caribbean call and response signing on and off contained in 'Tim Tim' and the ubiquitous 'story end and the wire bend', respectively to open and close a story. In the Igbo tradition, for example, Egudu and Nwoga describe the inter-relationship of audience and performer awareness and its importance to performance thus: "The spirit has to be on the ascendant for certain songs to be performed. On one ...occasion, the group refused to perform one of the most popular satirical songs because the dance 'was not yet properly cooked'; it had not reached the right pitch of excitement which would liberate their spirit and body to perform it right. Their apprehension was justified, for when later it was performed the audience were completely taken out of themselves and ...were thoroughly immersed in the mood of the song. One is likely to hear reactions like 'O hitele!' (...it is heated up) and 'akwasa!' ". (Egudu and Nwoga, 1971, p. 3).

The tradition of audience participation is such that political interpretation of superiority and subordination provide commonplace readings by the audience into what, to a Western ear are apparently innocuous tales. This can be at extreme cost to the authority of the storyteller should he or she impart the 'wrong' nuance. (Chukwuma, 1981, p.13).

Time

There is a close connection between audience and time in that an essential characteristic of performance has to be the present tense, a story is a live event happening now. The recipient has to be literally within earshot. It could appear that technological developments weaken the case for distinguishing too firmly between orality and text and so seem to offer implicit support to continuum theory. Records, tape and videos, prima facie, suggest effortless and instantaneous movement from one tradition to another. Indeed, without distinguishing the type of audience, this is the movement that Paul Keens-Douglas suggests that the audience makes. He has noted: "the biggest way to reach Caribbean audiences, still is through records, the ears, because we love to listen, we don't like to read. But listening encourages you to go out and buy the book. I sell more books through records, because people hear the story on the record and they go out and buy the book." (Keens-Douglas, 1984, p. 11).

The audience at a performance, however, is different. It is carrying out a different role, which involves a different kind of listening. Morris identifies this distinction when he notes, that the item that is being transferred through technology is an 'idea' or 'indication' of performance because, as he succinctly states, "we can never put the performance into print." (Morris, 1989, p.3).

Word power and 'tricks'

Different types of word power divide orality and text. It is useful here to illustrate the difference by drawing a distinction between power "of" the word (the oral context) and power "over" the word (the scribal context). Power over the word utilises verisimilitude and scribal prosody to form in its own terms the image that it seeks to create. In a discussion of creole in literature, Figueroa captures the essence of this exercise in his assertion: "Just as some paintings open for us a window on to the world...take us outside as it were....and some bring the world into us; so a writer of a sonnet with but fourteen lines, can open the window and take us outside, or bring the wide world, or the patterned garden, into our small room... even if we find the fragrance hurts. The poet has only language to do all this, and if he is wise he nurtures the varieties he knows and he fears not to use the whole of his repertoire." (Figueroa, 1989, p.7).

The importance of the power "of" the word in Caribbean society has been illustrated by Keens-Douglas both negatively, when it is denied, and positively, when it becomes, for example, through spoken humour, a mechanism of survival.

In 1984, he illustrated in a lecture how the power of the word has been neglected by the Caribbean media in its failure to use terms 'our people understand'. The authors of communication, he suggests, tend to ignore the fact that they are talking to 'dialect' people. He noted, for example, that: "Our radio and television is mainly to broadcast to our people so it should be in the kind of terms that our people can understand. But we put it in terms as if we are broadcasting to the rest of the world. Let the rest of the world make the effort to understand us. If they are really interested they will very well come down and understand what we are saying. But instead of that we change everything we have so that they can understand and we confuse our own people." (Caribbean Contact, 1984, p. 11).

The use of humour to express the most sombre mood at the graveside illustrates, in another vein, the power of the word: 'when we make a joke we are not really making a joke. Its use is far deeper.' Thus: "when you go to a funeral and people jump down in the grave and start to cry, they sorry for the person, and they crying and carrying on, but when they go home they say, "We had a great funeral, we enjoy ourselves, send on the person nice." It doesn't mean they don't miss the person or they don't think it is a sad occasion, but that is their way of expressing' (themselves). (Caribbean Contact, 1984, p. 15).

As an art form 'true' orality has long used tricks and humour to set alight the power 'of' the word. From 'Odysseus' ' defeat of the Cyclops to Anancy's traditional survival by cunning, these stories, in each instance invariably turn on word play. The strategy is also common among contemporary Caribbean performance poets, from Bennett's question about Miss Matty's desire to return to Africa:

"Yuh noh know wha yuh day-sey
Yuh haffe come from some weh fus
Before yuh go back deh?" (Bennett: 1986, p.31)
to Keens-Douglas' request to:
.... "Tell me again
how oil don't spoil,
how we have plenty dollars
but no sense,
and how money is no problem
but de problem is no money,
tell me again." (Burnett, 1986)

Both artists adopt two strategies of 'true' orality, a reliance on word-play as well as making jokes about 'serious' things.

Conclusion

This essay has sought to distinguish two forms of orality. These I have identified as 'true' and 'circumstantial' orality. 'True' orality is defined as having an identifiable epistemology and 'circumstantial' orality suggests the importance of performance and memorisation supported by a number of identifiable characteristics. Three that are referred to here are audience, time and the exercise of the power 'of' the word.

Two implications suggested by this argument are that in scribally dominated societies like the Anglo-phone Caribbean, 'true' orality is less apparent and artistic claims to a close affinity with orality are perhaps nearer to the artifice of orality.

Critics who are influenced by continuum theory have been concerned to develop an all embracing framework to incorporate and explain the diversity of Caribbean art forms, language and society. Such a framework perhaps underestimates important boundaries between scribal and oral art forms.

Prosody and Literary Texts

Femi Oyebode

'For a long, long time the human voice was the foundation of literature.... Then came the day when people knew how to read with their eyes, without spelling out the words, without hearing, and literature was thereby entirely altered.'

Paul Valery [1]

I want to argue that what is lost from literary texts is prosody; and I mean by this the loss of the articulation and ornamentation of speech by such devices as pitch, tone, rhythm, tempo, melody and harmony. I will argue that these devices are crucial to oral poetry. Indeed, oral poetry cannot exist, cannot communicate or express any meaningful emotion or idea without the raft which these devices lend it. I will argue that poetical texts are particularly afflicted in a severe way by this loss; the texts are dead whereas the voice in oral poetry is alive and vibrant.

The purpose of my argument is twofold: I wish to draw attention to the fact that when oral performances are transcribed, there is at least a need for a notation of prosody if not for a notation of the gestures and movement of the poet or for the responsive noises of the audience. I also wish to signify that the contribution of the African poet, writing in English, to the language must include an infusion of elements of speech derived from these prosodic devices. There is at present an overemphasis upon the introduction of unusual imagery or of unusual use of words. The deepest aspects of language, the capacity of poetry to inhabit the interface between pure music and prosaic speech and thereby to alter feelings, sensibility and belief by resonating with that quarter where the spirit resides like a stringed instrument waiting to be played, are least invoked.

1. Pitch

In Yorùbá poetry, pitch amongst other elements defines the type of poetry in question. The acuteness of the voice establishes whether the poetry is ijala, ifa, ofo, ewi, oriki, ogede or rara. Pitch therefore distinguishes between types much in the same way as number of syllables establishes that a particular text is an example of haiku, or the number of lines and metric form characterises a sonnet. This difference of approach demonstrates that the ear and not the eye is the principal judge of poetry, of oral poetry that is. If an ijala text was to be read in the same pitch as ogede it would cease to be ijala; the error would be as profound as rendering the blues in the style of an operatic aria.

The act of performing any of these particular forms of oral poetry is labelled differently in the language. For instance we would say sun ijala (sing ijala); pofo (called ofo); kewi (shouted/cried ewi); ki oriki (recite); sun rara (sing). These examples show that there is no unitary way of reciting poetry but rather that particular forms determine the style of recitation. Here, my use of the word 'recitation' is a misdescription of what happens. Quite often poetry is created in performance.

2. Tone

The tone of a text has become a synonym for the author's voice, the author's mannerisms of speech. Tone is therefore like the stride pattern, the cadence which a long distance runner habitually uses; like his gait and posture, the flowing outlines of his running frame defines him as distinct from others. The important point here is that the distinctiveness of one author from another is essential. We live in a culture which prizes individuation and no where is this more apparent than in literary texts. There is a perceived need to characterise the existence of a particular text or set of texts as belonging to a named author. Authorship implies particular rights and there are derivative obligations. It imposes upon the author the stricture of stylistic uniformity, and of conceptual and theoretical coherence. These strictures which are used to determine the quality of given texts are not value free. Indeed, it is quite easy to conjecture a set of rules which defines excellence as including the ability to masquerade in differing styles. The absence of the author from his work which Foucault[2] described as the defining character of authorship in our age is no longer true; Philip Roth has ensured that the life of the author is lived in the pages of his works. In truth, the author was never actually ever absent from the text, he only disguised his presence. This presence was signified by his tone. Change in tone was often perceived by critics as a weakness or a sign or immaturity; the poet was thought of as not having found his voice. Tone is communicated in texts by linguistic mannerisms and choice of words. For example, Philip Larkin,[3] (who an African poet can no longer read dispassionately) in This Be The Verse wrote 'They fuck you up, your mum and dad,/ They may not mean to, but they do./ They fill you with the faults they had/ And add some extra, just for you.' He communicated his rueful and comic tone by his use of coarse language and his turn of phrasing and the unexpected last line. The content therefore suggests how and in what tone to read this poem. The music and tone of this poem as Eliot[4] would have said are intrinsic and 'latent in the common speech of its time'. Compare this to Langston Hughes' Porter[5]: 'I must say/ Yes, sir,/ To you all the time./ Yes, sir!/ Yes, sir!/ All my days/ Climbing up a great big mountain/ Of yes, sirs!' The emotional tone which Hughes is trying to communicate is obvious enough. Yet, the music, the tone is elusive. This, I believe to be because Hughes is closer to an oral tradition than Larkin; Hughes does not use linguistic/textual means to communicate tone, he relies on the voice, the spoken voice to carry his frustrations, his quietly self-denigrating humour, his attack upon the masters. Hughes' poetry is for me a prime example of the failure of text to capture nuance and complexity.

In music, the tone which any individual produces from a particular instrument is personal and recognisably so. It was often said of Louis Armstrong that he was the only trumpet player of his time whose tone was entirely unabrasive in the whole range of the trumpet; 'one never felt the need to close one's ears to him'. How this was achieved technically is unclear, but it must have included such aspects as the size and shape of his lips, the pressure of his lips on the mouth piece, the force with which he blew and his capacity to modulate and control his breath. In literature too, tone can be intensely personal. And, in oral poetry, tone is as personal and distinctive as the singing voice. Linguistic devices become secondary; paralinguistic devices shape the meaning of words. In this way oral poetry is as close to drama and music as is possible.

3.   Rhythm and Tempo

The rhythm of a poetical text is denoted by its meter, the regular system of the alternation of accented and unaccented syllables. In English the length of the syllables do not appear to influence the construction of meter, whereas, in Greek and Latin the length of the syllables was the determining factor in meter. The function of rhythm is to give shape and coherence to successive lines, to pace the delivery and to institute a regularity which tunes the audience into the inner organisation of the poem. It is of great significance that the study of meter is called scansion; this term properly describes the scanning movement of the eye in seeking the rhythmical breaks in the lines. What the eye cannot register are the variations in pause length, in vowel length, in tempo and in facial and hand gestures which communicate the length of phrases and the timing of sub-clauses.

Much of contemporary poetry in English is written in regular meter. The use of irregular meter and the sprung rhythm of Hopkins is rare. Sprung rhythm is actually a term which acknowledges that pauses, properly timed are part of the construction of meter (these pauses are of course not notated in the text). Regular meter has a monotonic quality to the African ear; there is a felt need to alter the rhythm both within lines and between lines probably because the African ear demands rhythmic complexity. This tendency is evident in Osundare's poetry and in the case of Ben Okri induced one of the reviewers of his poetry to remark that there was no sense to his line breaks (this reviewer had failed to see/hear the inner rhythm of Okri's poetry). What is unusual in both writers is their combination of iambic and amphibrachic meters in the same lines; the amphibrachic meter is often constructed out of a pause, an accented short length middle syllable and a final weakly accented syllable.

Eliot[4] speaking of scansion said ' a study of anatomy will not teach you how to make a hen lay eggs' and I wish to add nor will it teach you how to hear poetry. Texts are impoverished documents which are lacking in the very essence of what poetry is about; rhythm, tempo and movement.

4.   Melody and Harmony

In a tonal language like Yorùbá , poetry can demonstrably have a melodic line which is distinct from the words and the meaning of the line. The melody or tune can be hummed and the aesthetic quality of this melody can be determined for better or worse just as one does for a piece of music. In this context, harmony refers to the way that successive notes fit aesthetically together. This is achieved not only by vowel harmonies or assonance but also by the relationship of the actual notes, the tones of the words to one another. There is no readily available equivalent of this aspect of Yorùbá poetry in the English language. This is not to say that English poetry is devoid of music, but only to remark that every 'language imposes its own laws and restrictions and permits its own licence, dictates its own speech rhythms and sound patterns'[4].

Mood is captured by the melodic line and De la Mare excels at this. He is able to balance each line against the next, distributing soft and harsh tones, long syllables and short, half-rhymes and internal rhymes with elegance and an acute ear for harmony: 'She will not die, they say,/ She will but put her beauty by/ And hie away'[6]. It is only Dennis Brutus, of contemporary African poets, who approaches de La Mere in his capacity to understand not only the semantic aspects of the language but also the essential music of the words. He too is able not 'to make use of all possible words, for among them are rare and baroque words which will attract all the attention to themselves and, in their vanity shine at the expense of thought'[7]: 'These are not images to cheer you/ - except that you may see in these small acts/ some evidence of my thought and caring:/ but still I do not fear their power to wound/ knowing your grief, your loss and anxious care..' [8]

Conclusion

'Music creates order out of chaos; for rhythm imposes unanimity upon the divergent; melody imposes continuity on the disjointed; and harmony imposes compatibility on the incongruous'. That is Yehudi Menuhin talking about the appeal of music. He could easily have been referring to oral poetry. The text only lives through the human voice.

1   Valery 1950.
2   Foucault 1977.
3   Larkin 1974.
4   Eliot 1942.
5   Hughes 1959.
6   Walter De la Mare 1918.
7   Valery 1927.
8   Brutus 1973.

Orality - (Theory) - Textuality: Tutuola, Okri, and the relationship of literary practice to oral traditions

Ato Quayson

> *'I thought you were a solid Christian,*
> *sir.' Stoll could not resist the jibe, 'But*
> *I see you're partial to all the fables.'*
> Wilson Harris, *The Secret Ladder*

General discussions of the relationship between orality and African literature often seem to ignore important questions as to the nature of both the oral traditions and of the literature in which those traditions are seen to operate. Frequently, as Karin Barber points out in her essay entitled "African-Language Literature and Post-Colonial Criticism,"[1] the discussions subtly bracket out the contexts of orality and valorise the literary. This tendency is particularly evident in the early surveys of African literature in Europhone languages in which the general move was from comments on oral literature to analyses of the literary productions of early African writers.[2] This tendency, she points out, persists even in contemporary post-colonial theory exemplified in works such as *The Empire Writes Back*, with its notion of Europhone post-colonial literature as being the arena in which the empire "writes" back to the centre and continually subverts the centre/margin dialectic. But there are several other implicit assumptions about the relationship between orality and literature which persist and need to be examined. Many of the issues around the relationship between the two modes have been raised in terms of anthropological paradigms. A notable early example was Emmanuel Obiechina's *Tradition, Culture and Society in the West African Novel* in which there was a sustained attempt to explore the novels in terms of their anthropological content and their representations of the regional culture and society. Though other critics have not been that explicit in their deployment of anthropological paradigms, the tendency has tacitly persisted and has become even more pronounced with the literary turn in contemporary anthropology and with its absorption by critics of African literature to raise new questions and propose fresh methods of analysis. An engagement with the debates around orality and African literature needs to look at some of the issues and methods raised by contemporary anthropology to assess its possible impact and also to clear a space for posing further questions at an interdisciplinary conjuncture. This paper will therefore situate itself at the intersection between anthropology and literary theory to contextualize a discussion of the works of Amos Tutuola and Ben Okri and the relationships they establish with traditional oral resources and to each other.

I

In a survey of anthropological theory since the sixties undertaken in 1984.
Sherry B. Ortner suggests that a new symbol of theoretical orientation is emerging
which may be labelled ' "practice" (or "action" or "praxis")'. Says he: 'This is
neither a theory nor a method in itself, but rather, as I said, a symbol, in the name
of which a variety of theories and methods are being developed' (Ortner, 127). It is
interesting that he uses the term "symbol" to describe the perceived theoretical
crisis at the heart of anthropology, for it reveals the current tendency in the
discipline to draw from literary paradigms for the explication of its own objects of
study. The suggestion of polysemy and indeterminacy that the term "symbol"
throws up is noteworthy as is the fact that the theoretical crisis is precisely due to
the interdisciplinary refocuses going on in the discipline. And the wealth of
suggestiveness inherent in this interdisciplinary crossing is perhaps best captured
in the programmatic discourse of the new anthropology featured in Clifford and
Marcus's *Writing Culture*.

Writing Culture is particularly interesting for its advocacy of the principle of
Bakhtinian dialogism in the writing of ethnographies. For as Clifford argues in the
introduction to the collection, the principle of dialogical textual production 'locates
cultural interpretations in many sorts of reciprocal contexts, and it obliges writers
to find diverse ways of rendering negotiated realities as multi-subjective, power-
laden and incongruent' (*Writing Culture*, 14). All this relates to an increasing
consciousness of the erosion of the ethnographer's authority and the consequent
necessity to re-negotiate that authority in engaging with the complexity of other
people's culture. But it seems to me that the principle of dialogism is far from
being exhausted and that, in fact, its invocation in certain contexts masks the
persistence of thoroughly monological and conservative attitudes towards other
people's cultures and cultural productions.[3] Something of this uneasy masking is
evident in Christopher Miller's much acclaimed *Theories of Africans* (TA)
published in 1990. This book is important partly because of the wide range of
issues it raises around orality, literacy and textual production and partly because
of the sophisticated way in which it engages with critical theory to authorise its
own critical discourse.

Miller starts off by pointing out the dangers of ethnocentrism involved in the
meeting between the Western critic and other people's cultures. The solution to
this problem is two-fold. Firstly, the Western critic requires an engagement with
the pronouncements of Africans on their literatures and cultures. 'Responsible
critics,' says Miller 'will no longer be able to ignore the mediation and authority of
African commentaries, critiques, and theoretical models, no more than in the past

they seemed able to ignore the so-called universal standards of Western judgement' (TA, 4). This cannot be said to be a spectacular proposition in itself since no self-respecting Western critic has dared to ignore the pronouncements of Africans on their own worlds. The important thing is *how* this engagement is undertaken and what discursive position the African theories are accorded. Miller's second proposition for negotiating the dangers of Western ethnocentricism is a thorough 'engagement with and dependence on anthropology' (TA, 4). He is however careful to repudiate the ethno-philosophy and anthropology of writers like Father Tempels and others who seek to essentialise African cultures and to see them as homogeneous and amenable to absorption within discursive structures that underprivilege them. To avoid these dangers, he advocates a conversion of discourse from totalization to dialogism (TA, 25-27). After engaging with the positions in *Writing Culture* and showing some of their loopholes, he goes on to assert that even if dialogue and freedom 'prove difficult or unattainable in the final analysis,' they remain 'the most compelling ethical models for the representation of cultures' (TA, 28).

His concerns are noble enough but it is when he comes to a practical consideration of certain critical issues that his principle of dialogism is found unsatisfactory. His second chapter, entitled "Ethnicity and Ethics" is significant in this respect. In it he attempts to explore the various applications of the concept of ethnicity by several African commentators on African literatures and cultures. In doing this, however, he establishes an opposition between "ethnicity" and "ethics" which is not sustainable and leads to strange complications. He first places theories such as Senghor's Negritude, Jahn's Muntu, and Soyinka's *Myth, Literature and the African World* under the rubric of ethnicity (TA, 33). This is somewhat strange, however, for in spite of their perceivable tendency towards essentialising African cultures, these discourses are best perceived as racialist Pan-Africanist theories and not local ethnic ones.[4] By invoking racialist models as ethnic ones, Miller subtly precludes a discussion of race from the analysis of the self/other problematic and also conceptually "detonates" potentially incendiary theories of difference to make way for an easier space from which to explore the problematic of analysing African literature and culture.

The category of ethics is also strangely constituted. Focusing on the high moral ground taken by African Marxists he conflates the concept of ethics with the Marxist category of class consciousness as exemplified in Gugelberger's *Marxism and African Literature* (TA, 35-41). He points out that African Marxism generally precludes analyses of pre-colonial traditions because of the dangers inherent in their invocation for the growth of class-consciousness. He then proceeds to deconstruct this "ethical" discourse of African Marxists by showing its consequences in the discourse of Frantz Fanon and the practice that derives from Fanon's theoretical categories when they are applied in Sekou Touré's Guinea. The focus on Sekou Touré is justified by the special place he and his first Minister of the Interior, Keita Fodéba, seem to take in Fanon's *Wretched of the Earth*, in which Touré is favourably quoted several times and Keita Fodéba's poetry is cited for analysis. It is to Sekou Touré's progressive estrangement from his people and the regression into totalitarianism that Miller points. He suggests explicitly that Fanon's essays share responsibility for the totalitarianism of Touré's regime:

> Fanon's essays had a part to play both in Touré's discourse
> and in his actions, providing a theoretical basis for relativizing
> truth and ethics (TA, 63).

The impression that this gives of the absolutely contaminating power of textual discourse irrespective of mediating circumstances is too loud to go unnoticed. But what is even stranger is the fact that this interpretation does not address the issue of how to theorise the practice of other African tyrants who cannot be shown to have any knowledge of Fanon such as Eyadema, Idi Amin, Mobutu and Kamuzu Banda. Are we to suppose that such tyrants were also captives of some textual discourses by which they justified their reckless tyranny? And it must also be noticed that by this stage in Miller's argument, the category of "ethics" has undergone a slippage away from its previous conflation with the Marxist category of class consciousness towards a purely moral usage. This is because he seeks to appropriate its more positive aspects for his own critical practice. The way has been prepared for a definition of an ethical critical practice:

> What is ethical would be a dialectical relationship between a
> transcendental truth and respect for the other, for difference.
> A self relating to itself has few ethical problems. In this sense,
> *there is no real ethics without ethnicity*, without the
> disquieting, untidy presence of the other (TA, 63).

We are left in doubt as to the constitution of the envisaged "transcendental truth," and what is meant by a "dialectical relationship" between that and respect for the Other is left to our fertile imaginations. But when we realise in subsequent chapters that he defines the purview of orality as in the broadest sense representative of 'the authenticity of the pre-colonial world' (TA, 70-71) the purview of his ethnicity paradigm and the emphasis of his critical project become clear. Miller seeks to engage with a sanitised ethnicity, to plough an African pre-colonial past amenable to a Western gaze and to show that it is indeed ethnical for the Western critic to focus on such a category. In establishing this, he also seeks to reduce the incendiary potential inherent in certain racialist theories and to discredit the high moral ground on which other critical discourses such as

Marxism have stood. His nuanced argumentation can be seen as masking the desire for an unproblematic Other in the guise of a dialogical embrace. As Uzo Ensowanne has rightly pointed out in a sharp critique of Miller's general position, his intervention on behalf of literary anthropology 'marks the restoration of the dimension of the dominance of scholastic investigations into Africa's immobilised antiquity over the volatile and fragmented realities of contemporary neo-colonial African nation-states' (Ensowanne, 116).

Perhaps what we see as Christopher Miller's conundrums are really the affliction of the field of anthropology and of notions of representation in the West in general. It is a crisis which dates to the crumbling of empire and which has been heightened by the criticism of Western philosophy generated from within the West itself. It seems, however, that this crisis in consciousness in relation to the representation of the Other has been negotiated mainly by refining the self/other dialectic in the direction of shifting focus away from the observed and onto the observer. This explains the general concern in *Writing Culture* with the representational status of ethnographies and the problematic of the ethnographic I/eye. For the collaborators in *Writing Culture*, the principle of Bakhtinian dialogism becomes a welcome method by which the *textual* representation of cultures is undertaken, leading to an envisaged freeing of hitherto stilled voices to be represented in scientific ethnographies. But this shift has the subtle and not too happy effect of problematising textual representation while leaving the object observed, that is culture, relatively untouched. This allows the persistence of certain homogenising tendencies as evidenced in the work of Christopher Miller even as he seriously engages with questions of how to represent the Other.[5]

For my part, I propose to focus on the constitution of the object of study itself, in this case traditional Yorùbá culture, to propose ways in which it can be described and related to the work of Okri and Tutuola. After Hountondji's critical interventions in the arena of African philosophy, it is now no longer viable to engage in homogenising statements about African cultures even from the position of a native. As Hountondji points out, when the word "philosophy" is applied to African systems of thought, it is often used to designate a collective world-view, an implicit, spontaneous and perhaps even unconscious system of beliefs to which all Africans adhere. Behind this he detects a myth at work, the myth of "primitive unanimity" in which everyone is in harmonious agreement with everyone else (Hountondji, 60-62). He is rightly impatient with this type of thinking. But what he asserts as the special constitution of the philosophy of books (and of any science for that matter) in which the governing paradigm is free discussion and the confrontation of hypotheses and theories created or assumed by the thoughts of individuals and located within historical processes, is in fact within the purview of traditional cultures themselves. Of course, the manner by which traditional cultures create and maintain a rich interchange of ideas differs from what obtains in scientific discourse, and there is no desire for cultures to aspire to the neatness of science. But it is the homogeniser's gaze that stabilises the rich discursivity and interplay of meanings inherent in traditional cultures and that institutes an unbridgeable rupture between the discourses of orality and those of science such that philosopher's like Hountondji can only regard Africanist discourse as reprehensibly simplistic and unscientific.

Yorùbá culture, when studied closely, reveals a rich and variegated picture. The first thing to note is that in Yorùbá traditional culture, the oral traditions are far from homogeneous and are in a constant process of transformation. Each of the major Yorùbá groupings has an active relationship to the various oral genres that circulate among them, and it is perhaps best to speak of a model of discursive dialogism governing both the genres and the uses to which they are put. The processes of this dialogism are inscribed within the heart of the totality of the culture itself and emerge in the relationship between past and present, between genre and genre, between speaker and speaker, and between the traditional resource base and the literatures written in both English and Yorùbá.

Robin Law (1973) has already noted how in Yorùbá culture the creation myths of Oduduwa have been deployed by various groupings to shore up their own claims to pre-eminent authority. Surely this is an important observation, but what is crucial to note is that it is not only political authorities or interest groupings that transform oral narrative materials to their specific uses; it is a feature of ordinary Yorùbá practice itself to maintain a constant re-creative engagement with oral narrative forms and oral traditions. This feature becomes better clarified when we recall Karin Barber's observations in "Multiple Discourses in Yorùbá Oral Literature" about the different oral genres in Yorùbáland. In an analysis of the varying relationships between *ese Ifá* (Ifa divination verses), *àló* (folktales) and *oríkì* (praise poetry and appellations), Barber notes that Yorùbá oral genres are generally marked by a high level of 'porosity and incorporativeness.' Not only are there multiple, overlapping and partly incompatible discourses, but 'the proliferation of alternative perspectives, the holding open of possibilities, the deferral of final ideological resolution, is itself a dominant value' (Barber, 13). She tries to show how the same narrative materials are often absorbed by each genre and refocalised for different purposes by the other genres in question. In that case the relationship between the genres is itself one of a constant dialogical interplay and discursive exchange making it difficult to make hasty totalizing statements about Yorùbá oral traditions. The re-focusing of the Oduduwa myth that Law observes can then be taken to be a constant feature of the oral traditions in general. Of course it is necessary to note that this refocusing often goes with an articulation of power and authority, especially in the genres used mainly by institutionally influential groups such as the *babalawo* (Ifa divination priests), the *Arókin* (court historians), hunters groups and other groups and figures. But the interesting thing is that there seems to be a constant process within the culture of re-appropriation and therefore of undermining any monological application of the contents of any genre.

All this leads to the consideration of another significant issue in relation to orality and oral traditions in the Yorùbá context: the meaning(s) of the specific genres can only be grasped within their contexts of production. However, context of production should not be taken as coterminous with context of performance. For though the notion of context of performance is absolutely crucial for the analysis of genres within oral cultures, it can take on a limited application that can preclude other considerations.[6] The context of production, in a wider usage, would also include the socio-cultural context of those who participate in the performance of the discourse itself, their differing gender and power relations being as much a part of the interactive procedure that constitutes the context of performance. And the context of production would conceivably also include the relationship of the form in question to other oral narrative and poetic forms towards which they can be seen to gesture. It would also include the socio-political context of a wider Nigeria, since, it seems to me, the participants in the performance are also criss-crossed by other allegiances of a wide nature. The various threads of the oral genres have to be pursued backwards, forwards and sideways towards history, towards the immediate contexts of performance and towards other Yorùbá narrative genres.

If the notion of the incorporativeness and porosity of Yorùbá oral genres is kept in view the problem of negotiating the interface between these traditional resources and the literary writings of Nigerian writers leads us in various directions simultaneously. It becomes clear that when writers deploy oral traditions in their writings they are entering into a discursive engagement with orality for specific purposes. Though it is useful to read the writings of Tutuola and Okri and even of Soyinka and Achebe in conjunction with anthropological introductions to their respective cultures, it is necessary to remember that these literary writings are far from reflective surfaces faithfully capturing stable and homogeneous cultures. The question to ask is not how *true* a reflection of culture a literary text is but *what* purposes the cultural concepts and categories are serving within the literary universe. Following Eileen Julien, the question we must ask ourselves is what particular aesthetic and ideological problems the recourse to oral materials is meant to address in the context of African literature. For, as she rightly observes, 'the issue at hand is not the orality of Africa but rather the intellectual categories of orality and writing that we construct and use....[H]ow the category of "African orality" permeates literary criticism, how it is subject to ideological pressures, and how it has come to define and confine the scope of our interest in and perception of African writing' (Julien, 7). Clearly, the emphasis must be on examining "orality" and "writing" as constructed theoretical categories that have significant implications for the way in which the objects of study are perceived and spoken about.

In relation to Ben Okri's work, the question that I seek to address is what attitudes he reveals towards the traditional conceptual resources he draws upon for his novel *The Famished Road*. Since, as I have argued, the realm of traditional orality is far from stable, and the relationship of literary writing to oral traditions is often one of a discursive and strategic engagement, I shall seek to explore ways in which he deploys traditional concepts and how he transforms them so as to address issues of contemporary relevance. To engage with these questions, I propose to raise Amos Tutuola as a contrastive analogue to Ben Okri to show how several of Tutuola's traditional concepts are taken up and transformed by Okri. I bear in mind the fact that Okri is not a Yorùbá at all and that it is arguable that the concepts he deploys have nothing to do with the paradigms Tutuola deploys in his own narratives. However, I still think it is useful to raise Tutuola's work in comparison with Okri's partly because it is impossible to read Okri without remembering Tutuola[7] and also because such a comparison may happily lead to a radical reconsideration of the concept of ethnicity in general, since it is increasingly evident that Africans operate multiple ethnicities all their lives, this becoming more pronounced when they are brought up in cosmopolitan environments such as Lagos, Accra or Nairobi.[8] Furthermore, it seems plausible now to propose a model of interpretation which would relate African novels simultaneously to putative contexts of orality as well as to other literary texts with which they can be shown to be related conceptually.

The relationships between specific literary texts and their putative contexts of orality and to each other need not be traced just in terms of evident motifs and images as has generally characterised the criticism of writers such as Achebe and Soyinka. It is also possible to trace these relationships in terms of wider conceptual paradigms and ideas. I shall attempt to outline such a critical model by relating Tutuola and Okri to each other and to their traditional resource base in terms of some of the concepts that are played out in their texts. This model seems increasingly viable because of the creative activity that continually goes on in the Nigerian context of literary production and that conceivably comprehends a growing dialogism among the various literary texts.

II

Amos Tutuola

Amos Tutuola's first two works were a sort of literary bombshell both in Africa and in the West, and though he went on to write more works in the same vein, his first two books seem to be the best known of his output. It is on these two that we shall focus, partly for reasons of their popularity and also because it is these two that seem to shed greatest light on Okri's own practice. The first issue that *The Palm-Wine Drinkard* (PWD) and *My Life in the Bush of Ghosts* (LBG) threw up was that of categorisation. Though Tutuola had been published in book form it was evident that he was reproducing Yorùbá folk narratives. This led to a rather cool reception from West Africans. As one critic put it: '[Tutuola] merely translates in a literal fashion from the Yorùbá in which all the old legends are still verbally told' (Lindfors 1980: 27). In separate interviews Tutuola himself says that he had always been interested in telling and listening to folk stories and that he began writing partly because 'it seemed necessary to write down the tales of my country since they will soon all be forgotten' (Lindfors, 1980: 229). The plot and content of his narratives bear out this traditional resource base, and show that he is in a discursive relationship with oral narrative genres.[9]

The Palm-Wine Drinkard is about a man who goes into the underworld to search for his dead palm-wine tapster. In the quest for the tapster he goes through a lot of adventures fighting with the denizens of the spirit-world, the majority of whom take a violent attitude to him. The protagonist finally meets the tapster in one of the towns, but he refuses to return with him. He instead gives him a magic egg with which the hero returns to solve certain important communal crises. *My Life in the Bush of Ghosts* (BG), on the other hand, is about a seven-year old who, in escaping the gunfire of a tribal war, enters into the bush of ghosts. In the search for a way home he travels through a number of ghost towns, encounters a wide range of terrifying spirits, marries twice, learns the language of ghosts and after duels with a ghost-magician and certain acts of goodwill, he returns home to laughter and tears. Heroes are often composite-creations made up of the most popular folk protagonists such as the hunter, the jujuman, the trickster and the superman. Many of the adventures he relates closely resemble well known Yorùbá yarns, but his stories are usually a collage of both borrowed and self-created materials put together in an eclectic manner with very interesting imaginative embellishments imposed on the whole. Critics such as Gerald Moore have examined his stories in terms of the universal monomyths of Departure, Initiation and Return and have suggested that Tutuola has affinities with Bunyan and Dante. Others have seen him in the light of Northrop Frye's narrative topoi and have suggested that his works be regarded as "naive romances"[10]. For my own purposes, I want to focus on certain aspects of his stories from which we can make tentative suggestions as to the encoding of certain concepts that are later reproduced and problematized in Okri's work.

(a) The first thing to note is that in his first two works there is a strong notion of the hero crossing a threshold before entering into the realm of spirit adventures. In *The Palm-Wine Drinkard* the boundary is blurred at the point of entry, but it becomes clearly evident when the Drinkard is departing the other world. He is given a hot chase by a number of "mountain ghosts" but transforms himself into a pebble to elude them. He bounces along just ahead of them till they reach a river that lies across the way home. The Drinkard, still a pebble, bounces across and is immediately free from pursuit because the "mountain spirits" are incapable of crossing this all-important river. In *My Life in the Bush of Ghosts* the boundary is clear from the start. The seven-year old protagonist, running away from the ravages of a tribal war, enters the realm of ghosts by crossing such a boundary, though he is at the time unconscious of it. Says he:

> But as the noises of the enemies guns drove me very far until I entered in the "Bush of Ghosts" unnoticed because I was too young to know that it was a dreadful bush or it was banned to be entered by earthly person...(BG, 22)

The Tutuolan tales seem to be analogous to initiation rites especially as described by Van Gennep (1908). Van Gennep divides the rituals of rites of passage into the three phases of *separation, transition* and *reabsorption*. These phases are conceptually defined as the *pre-liminal*, the *liminal* and the *post-liminal* respectively. It is in the area of the liminal that the beneficiaries of initiation are schooled into the mores of the society. Victor Turner (1969) expands on Gennep's central concepts and adds that the area of the liminal is an area of anti-structure and ambiguity. It is an area which involves the conceptual denuding of initiates to establish a sense of community and equality before a reabsorption into the society can take place. It is important to note, however, that the folktale as exemplified in Tutuola's use of it has recourse to a different signification of the liminal phase. The spirit threshold, in the general context of Tutuola's tales, is a zone of liminality and reveals a strong sense of anxiety at crossing the boundary between the real world and the world of spirits. In Yorùbáland, as in much of Africa, the spirit world of the ancestors and the gods is accessed through special rituals. There seems to be a clear danger inherent in crossing into the spirit world without proper preparation through ritual. Within the folktale however, the person who crosses that boundary becomes an immediate centre of potential meanings. In these narratives the passage through the liminal zone seems to be a process towards greater empowerment. The violent adventures that Tutuola's characters undergo can all be seen as a process of affirming the problematic status of the protagonist because of their entry into the world of spirits. And as the protagonists progress through the various adventures they acquire a sort of empowerment which is one over and above that available in initiation rituals in general. The emphasis in the Tutuolan narratives seems to be on the heroism of the individual spirit against the elemental anxiety-generating forces running amok in the universe.

(b) Another aspect of Tutuola's stories of interest here is the frequency of character metamorphoses in the stories. In *The Palm-Wine Drinkard*, the protagonist among other things changes into a canoe, a bird and even a pebble. There are many more of such transformations in the *Bush of Ghosts* than in the *Palm-Wine Drinkard*. In one episode for instance, the young boy is captured by a powerful 'smelling-ghost' who decides to use him to show off his magical powers to other 'smelling-ghost' friends. This is what happens:

> In the presence of these guests, my boss was changing me to some kinds of creatures. First of all he changed me to a monkey, then I began to climb fruit trees and pluck fruits down for them. After that he changed me to a lion, then to a horse, to a camel, to a cow or bull with horns on its head and at last too my former self. (BG, 36)

He is later on changed to a horse and is ridden by the smelling-ghost for a number of days. After that the young boy manages to steal the smelling-ghost's medicine and transforms himself into a cow to escape his master. He falls into different hands and is sold to certain cultic adherents who wish to sacrifice him to a god. It is only good fortune that saves him from a very uncomfortable end. But it is important to note too that the protagonist is both a victim and a spectator of metamorphoses. Much later in the narrative, he marries a beautiful "Super Lady" who turns out to be the daughter of a powerful witch and a wizard. She demonstrates what powers she herself has inherited by changing very rapidly into different animals. She changes from an antelope with two short horns into a ferocious lioness and then into a huge boa constrictor which coils itself round the hero and makes as if to swallow him. She then changes into a tigress which springs out into the courtyard to chase and catch some chickens and then returns to the house to metamorphose back into a charming lady (BG, 118-19). Given the frequency of these metamorphoses the question is: What do they signify both as an element of Tutuola's discourse and of the values it encodes?

A partial answer to this question seems to be offered in one of the numerous transformation episodes in *My Life in the Bush of Ghosts*. The hero has his head mistakenly replaced by a ghost's head, having lost his own during a battle he fought on the side of one ghost town against another. The missing heads of all beheaded ghosts are replaced by a powerful ghost figure who resurrects all the dead ghosts and replaces their heads randomly. The hero is very unhappy with this new head, for, as he tells us:

> [E]very ghost is talkative, so this head was always making various noises both day and night and also smelling badly. Whether I was talking or not it would be talking out the words which I did not mean in my mind and was telling out all my secret aims which I was planning in mind...(BG, 109)

But when he complains that he is uncomfortable with this newly acquired head he is told that 'every head is a head and there is no head which is not suitable for any creature'. It seems, then, that the various metamorphoses are an important juncture at which the phenomenological variety of experience is explored. They become a special paradigm within the narratives which encapsulates certain concepts. Apart from comprehending the variety of natural phenomena, the paradigm of metamorphosis also involves in itself a sense of the crossing of boundaries. But this time the crossing is not just between two realms but between discrete phenomena *in* nature. It involves a perceived intersubjectivity at the hart of Nature. It is possible, within the context of the narratives, for men to inhabit the consciousness of animals, stones and other discrete phenomena. Additionally, this paradigm of metamorphosis embraces some measure of anxiety because of the strangeness that seems to inhere in the envisaged intersubjectivity between natural phenomena. Quite often, Tutuola's characters express uneasiness and alarm at inhabiting consciousnesses other than their own.

But perhaps this paradigm is an expression of a simultaneous sense of limitation in the face of the complexity of the cosmos and a transcending of that limitation even if only within the imaginative arena of the folktale. If we grant that Tutuola's narratives are a fair rendition of Yorùbá folktale narratives then perhaps the liminal phase in Yorùbá culture appears to be crossed not just once or in the context of specific ritual circumstances, but continually in the process of exploring the variety of natural phenomena within the imaginative arena of the folk narratives. Significantly, however, the traditional culture explores this problematic within a special space in the oral narrative forms by demarcating the real from the other-worldly and by suggesting that it is the movement from the one to the other that unleashes the fantastic and often frightening potential of the intersubjectivity inherent in Nature. Furthermore, there is another level of demarcation which is that constituted by the context of narration itself. Formulaic openings ensure that the oral narrative forms are marked so that they trigger certain expectations as to their conceptual modes of operation.[11] In this way, narratives such as those Tutuola reproduces are a means of exploring certain conceptions of Nature and of existence within the conceptually self-contained space of the traditional narratives themselves.

(c) The most important aspect of oral narratives seems to be the folktale characters themselves. As Ong (1982) points out, characterisation serves as a means of encoding the oral culture's value-system and also as a significant mnemonic device. In the *Palm-Wine Drinkard*, the protagonist has immense magical powers and at one point even brags that he is 'father of all the gods.' All his adventures serve to emphasise his powers. On the other hand, the hero of *My Life in the Bush of Ghosts* starts his journey through the bush as a powerless lad. He shows a resilient nature very early in his adventures, and he gradually acquires magical powers of his own. By the later parts of the book, he masters the language of ghosts, engages in a contest with a powerful magician and defeats him, and magically replaces the lost arm of a wife of the King of the 4th town of ghosts. He also heals a television-handed ghostess of sores that have covered her body for over two hundred years. Clearly the protagonists of these tales have great heroic stature. Their journeys through the ghost-worlds serve as a means of empowerment and all the adventures affirm a confidence in the ultimate triumph of the human spirit over the anxiety-generating forces that are seen to abound in the universe. And it is important to note that in these oral narratives, the unknown and anxiety-generating forces are encoded as horrible and grotesque creatures, partly in an effort to make them memorable and partly also to affirm the stature of the protagonist in defeating them.

Ben Okri

In The Famished Road (TFR), Okri establishes an interesting relationship with the resource base that Tutuola draws upon. But in Okri's work there seems to be a constant displacement of the concepts operative in Tutuola's work, so as to display a range of applications that extend to embrace ideological and aesthetic concerns of a different status from Tutuola's. For whereas Tutuola's narratives are concerned with reproducing the consistency of the traditional folktale universe, Okri's novel explores the viability of some of the traditional folktale concepts within contemporary real-world existence.

(a) We must note that in The Famished Road all the events are focalized through the eyes of Azaro, a participant narrator. He is a seven-year old abiku child who has undergone a series of rebirths, always dying at a young age and has finally decided to stay in the world to make his parents happy. He is thus a thoroughly liminal figure. A sense of the crossing of a threshold is also evident in this novel but there is an interesting inversion; this time the crossing is often from the spirit-world into the real world. Secondly, the sense of terror and foreboding at the crossing of liminal thresholds is replaced by a sense of loss and sadness at having to leave the idyllic world of spirit-companions to enter the real world.

Significantly, however, when that first threshold is crossed and Azaro enters the real world, a continuous intercourse is permanently established between the real world and that of spirits. Furthermore, the spirit-realms in the novel seem to be of different orders. On the one hand there is the idyllic world of his spirit companions who continually entice him to return to them. There is also a more harrowing spirit-world in which he often undergoes frightful experiences with various spirit-figures. What is important for our analysis is the fact that when in the real world, the spirit realms are entered into without any sense of the crossing of boundaries. The entries and exits are conducted within subtle narrative shifts that serve to dispense with all signals of a liminal boundary. The narrative is constructed out of a dense interweaving of "spirit" and "reality" passages and these are linked in various ways in terms of shifts within the narrative itself. At the risk of unduly schematising the range of linkages between the two realms, we will note their general characteristics:

1. Sometimes the shift from the reality-plane to the spirit or esoteric-plane is undertaken within the same geographical space in which that space is located simultaneously in both realms. An example is when he enters the "belly of the road" only to find out after a short sleep that it is in fact an excavated sand-pit (TFR, 15-18).

2. There are times also when it is Azaro who moves from one geographical setting to another, usually from home into the forest or market, and this serves as a trigger for the emergence of the spirit realm. This is a frequent occurrence.

3. At other times spirit figures emerge into the reality-plane to interact with real people, but they are usually recognised as spirits only by Azaro himself (TFR, 25-26, 297-304, 459-61).

4. At other times spirit-figures come into the reality-plane to transport Azaro to the spirit-realm, leading to its dominance in the narrative. Such for instance is the episode of his kidnapping by the cult of women and also his journey with the three-headed spirit into the underworld (TFR, 11-14, 325-39).

5. All these shifts are completely arbitrary. Azaro does not necessarily desire them and is completely at the mercy of the shifts in the narrative.

(b) Certain important implications derive from the specific interweaving of the reality and esoteric planes in *The Famished Road*. In the narrative shifts from the reality-plane to the esoteric plane in which the same space is simultaneously located within both realms, there is a suggestion that Azaro, and by implication the rest of nature and existence in general is on a continually shifting conceptual space and partly at the mercy of those shifts. This affects the general notion of time and space within which the notion of liminal thresholds and of transitions find their validity. The notion of liminal thresholds is no longer conceived of as a medial point within the process of transition from one status to another one of perhaps greater significance. These processes of transition are normally marked by acts of volition in the narrative space of the traditional folktale, and, within a larger cultural context, by acts of ritual self-preparation. The possibility of accessing the spirit world through ritual acts of volition or self-will are completely frustrated within the narrative of *The Famished Road*. And this is mainly because the shifts from one experiential plane to the next are no longer within the control of the central characters. Unlike what we saw operating in Tutuola's narratives, the spaces of reality and of the spirit-world are no longer demarcated so that men can move from one to the other through their own volition. The logic of arbitrary shifts seems to take precedence over the volitional acts of the central characters.

The linear experiential plane on which "this" and "an-other" are usually plotted is displaced here. Even Tutuola's narratives were governed by such a conceptual linearity, and as we would recall, his narratives always demarcated the real from the esoteric suggesting that it was only in the esoteric realm that fantastic events took place. In the mythopoeia of *The Famished Road*, it seems that the experience of the reality and esoteric planes is caught within interlocking circles in which both the circles and the natural phenomena caught within them are in continuous motion. In this mythopoeia, "this" and the "other" are in a permanent interactive co-existence. The notion of intersubjectivity that seems to have been captured in the Tutuolan narratives in terms of character metamorphoses has here been expanded to embrace the very constitution of both the real and the esoteric realms without demarcated spaces between them. It is as if to suggest that the state of intersubjectivity is the inseparable fusion of two different realms of existence and not just the interaction of discrete objective natural phenomena.

(c) The element of the grotesque, which in Tutuola's narratives attached to figures in the spirit-world, is here distributed among figures in both the reality and spirit planes. The spirit-characters in the novel are certainly very strange. There are, for instance, three- and two-headed spirits with heads of different colours. At one time Azaro encounters in the forest 'a creature ugly and magnificent like a prehistoric dragon, with the body of an elephant and the face of a warthog' (TFR, 243). At Madam Koto's bar, he encounters strange spirits who seem to have borrowed parts from human bodies to come into the real world. There is a man who has no thumbs and whose head, amazingly contorted like certain tubers of yam, is altogether bald. There is also a very tall man who has a disc-like eye inside his mouth. But it seems to me that some of the real characters he meets at various times on the reality plane can match any of the spirits in grotesqueness. Witness for instance the description of a lunatic whom Azaro meets at the market-place and who expresses an uncanny interest in a piece of bread he is holding:

> There was a man standing near me. I noticed him because of
> his smell. He wore a dirty, tattered shirt. His hair was reddish.
> Flies were noisy around his ears. His private parts showed
> through his underpants. His legs were covered in sores. The
> flies around his face made him look as if he had four eyes. I
> stared at him out of curiosity. He made a violent motion,
> scattering the flies, and I noticed that his two eyes rolled
> around as if in an extraordinary effort to see themselves.
> (TFR, 17)

The impression that this lunatic's eyes have undergone multiplication because of a swarm of flies is unsettling enough, but what is even more distressing is that his eyes, much like the flies that surround them, cannot keep still. A second lunatic is encountered in front of Madam Koto's bar. His description is also striking:

> He had only a pair of sad-looking underpants. His hair was
> rough and covered in a red liquid and bits of rubbish. He had
> a big sore on his back and a small one on his ear. Flies
> swarmed around him and he kept twitching. Every now and
> then he broke into a titter.
> . . . . He had one eye higher than another. His mouth was like
> a festering wound. He twitched, stamped, laughed and
> suddenly ran into the bar. (TFR, 84)

Once again we must take note of the queer nature of this man's eyes. And his mouth itself is like a festering wound, referring as much to its raw look as to the overpowering stench of putrefaction that can be thought to emanate from such a mouth. What we see operating in *The Famished Road* is that the grotesque and bizarre are now redistributed between both the spiritual and the real world so as to suggest that real-world existence shares in the absurdity of the "other". Furthermore, the anxiety-generating forces, which in the Tutuolan narratives were encoded as grotesque monsters in the special arena of the liminal spaces, are now a component of the real world.

(d) It seems, however, that the most significant change in the use of the mythopoeic resource base and the attitudes towards it is registered in the characterisation of the central character Azaro. Azaro has none of the heroic stature of the Tutuolan heroes. He has no access to magic or juju, and his esoteric experiences do not act as enabling initiations which would empower him to deal better with the exigencies of the real world. Rather, there is a sense in which he remains steadfastly ignorant of whatever power the status of *abiku* affords him. Several times other characters recognise his spiritual potential and attempt to harness it for their own ends. The cult of women kidnap him and take him to their island because they hope he will be "reborn" by their goddess who is pregnant and is in labour when he is brought. He is coaxed and kidnapped by other spirits at Madam Koto's bar, but he adopts a bland attitude to all their efforts. Madam Koto herself insists on having him come and sit in her shop with her after school. She offers to pay his school fees and to remit the debts owed her by his father. She thinks he will attract customers. This he does, but they turn out to be very different from the customers she expects.

Azaro's is not a heroism that involves combat with elemental forces; his condition is to *Be*, to exist the essence of an *abiku*, comprehending different realms simultaneously and utterly powerless to change the order of things. He himself offers us a key to understanding his condition, when, in describing the attack of thugs on his street he says that he perceived 'in the crack of a moment, the recurrence of things unresolved - histories, dreams, a vanished world of great old spirits, wild jungles, tigers with eyes of diamonds roaming the dense foliage' (TFR, 176). His condition is to see the recurrence of things within the flux of existence. The insights gained from his experience of the spirit world seem to remain unutilizable for Azaro within the frame of the real world, unlike in the case of Tutuola's heroes who often return with an enhanced capacity to deal with the exigencies of the real world. This impression is generated partly because the esoteric experiences do not operate within any discernible teleological framework. If there is any teleology, it can be seen not in terms of a linear progression, but rather in terms of the cyclical 'once and the repeated time' intimated by Wole Soyinka in his poem "Abiku".

Though the hero of *The Famished Road* partly exists within the numinous arena of the mythopoeic traditional folktale, the esoteric experiences are not an enabling rite of passage, in the sense that they can be perceived in Tutuola's narrative universe. Azaro's condition is thoroughly the *abiku's* condition, and it seems his lot is to be acutely aware of the circularity and intersubjectivity inherent in the two co-existing and interlocking planes of existence. In *The Famished Road*, there is the subtle suggestion that it is the experiences of the real world itself that constitute the rite of passage, though some significant inspiration can be drawn from an understanding of the spirit realm and its relationship to the real world.

In the novel the initiatory and empowering potential inherent in experience of the unusual seems to be allotted by the narrative to Azaro's father, a man firmly grounded in the struggles of the real world. From the very beginning Azaro's father, popularly known as the Black Tyger, is portrayed as a man full of energy burdened by the struggles imposed by an impoverished existence. He carries his burden with much grumbling and is not beyond outbursts of domestic violence. But at the same time there are subtle suggestions that his struggles against poverty border on a titanic struggle against elemental forces that would destroy man's soul. From the very early stages of the narrative, Azaro describes his father as a giant:

> That evening Dad became the guardian giant who lead me into
> the discoveries of our new world. We were surrounded by a
> great forest. (34)

The titanic qualities become most evident when he is angry; they show up for instance when he is enraged at his creditors' despicable seizure of his clothes and pieces of furniture in his absence:

> He growled like an enraged lion, drew himself up to his fullest
> titanic height, stormed out of the room, and began raging down
> the passage so loudly that it seemed as though thunder had
> descended among us. (96)

Indeed, the Black Tyger seems to have a special relationship to thunder in his son's eyes, and at another fight, this time in Madam Koto's bar, the association is made more explicitly:

> 'So what do you want to do?' the man asked, fingering his
> amulet. 'Do you know this thing I have here, eh? If you touch
> me you will fall down seven times and then...'

The braggart is not allowed to complete his sentence. Something fantastic happens:

> Suddenly - it seemed like a flash of lightning was lost in the
> bar - Dad had hit him in the face. It happened very fast. The
> next moment the bar door was wide open and the man had
> disappeared. We heard him groaning outside in the dark. The
> lightning vanished back into Dad's fist. (301)

These titanic references remain at the level of subtle suggestion, but work towards giving Azaro's father heroic stature even amidst his debilitating circumstances. His titanic stature is finally confirmed by his fight with the spirit of the Yellow Jaguar. If any doubts about his titanic stature have remained before this fight, they are rapidly dispelled when we see him defeat a "boxer" whose body felt like a tree and who had 'a mighty voice, speaking with the power of darkness' (TFR, 356).

The Black Tyger grows in the direction of a fuller realisation of the reality of the spirit world but from the arena of his worldly experiences. When he is training with his son in preparation for his bout with the Yellow Jaguar he undergoes a strange test of his charitable impulses by an old man who 'carries something invisible on his head.' Luckily he passes the test and the old man tells him how lucky he is. It is a very important experience for him and as he tells his son, he begins to see things clearly for the first time. The whole context of the fight with the spirit of Yellow Jaguar and the preparations towards it then become the final step in the affirmation of titanic stature for the Black Tyger. The process of initiation has been transferred from the usual folktale context of a series of spiritual encounters onto the processes of real world existence. It is not by accident that Azaro's father enters into a "prophetic" phase at the end of the novel. His espousal of a vision of peace on earth seems to be somewhat idealistic, but it has been acquired through harsh real-world experiences in addition to a grasp of the reality of the spirit world. But at the same time the Black Tyger's characterisation has something of the Yorùbá gods Shango and Ogun as subtexts, because his struggles against the threatening extinction that poverty and injustice pose recalls the two gods of Yorùbá mythology. If two types of heroism are thus presented, the novel seems to suggest the inadequacy of the former mode of characterisation within the folktale. For at the same time as the narrative privileges Azaro by making him the consciousness through which all the events are focalized, it also undermines his mode of signification by portraying his father as a more energetic and positive character. It is as if to suggest a fascination with the numinous mythopoeic potential of the hero of the folktale, with a progressive conceptual enervation attaching to its depiction to signal the problematic status of its signifying mode within the new literary and socio-political frame of reference.

What, then, can we say has been the purpose of Okri's deployment of certain concepts from the traditional resource base? In what ways can we discuss the interface between orality and literature in his particular case? And what particular contemporary concerns is he addressing? I can only venture tentative answers to these questions because of the inexhaustive nature of this paper. But it does seem to me that in deploying some of the concepts operative in Tutuola's narratives, Okri shows a certain rich ambivalence towards the traditional resource base. On the one hand there is a fascination for its potential for generating multiple focuses, but on the other hand, there is an acute sense of its inadequacy in addressing the pressures of an aesthetic facing the exigencies of a post-colonial reality that is cosmopolitan, in-between, and riddled by multiple identities.

The novel seems to address a second issue of profound significance, and that is the depiction of a resilient mode of traditional consciousness that is both mythopoeic and popular. It is interesting that the narrative is located in the urban ghetto, for it seems that it is the dwellers of the urban ghetto who most supremely activate this consciousness at the same time as they absorb the modes of perception of the modern world. The conditions of the urban ghetto can be said to be those of a liminal phase refracted in the material world of urban dispossession. For even as ghettos grow at the margins of cities absorbing the rural migrant population, they also encapsulate the persistence of multiple modes of self-conceptualisation. The dwellers of urban ghettos are constrained to a marginal existence at various levels, economic, political and socio-cultural. And because of the particular difficulties for upward mobility in the urban ghettos, the conditions of liminality ruthlessly persist over time. It is these conditions that generate the most nuanced understanding of the interface between oral traditions and modernity. The ideas of modernity are absorbed very rapidly, but traditional belief systems are continually activated to make meaning of the ghetto existence and to forge productive alliances. If Okri locates his work in the urban ghetto, he also emphasises its liminality by focalizing the life of the ghetto through the eyes of the liminal Azaro. The concepts in the traditional resource base have thus been deployed to heighten the ambiguities inherent in the dispossession of real world existence. Like the practitioners of orality, Okri has garnered the oral tradition's potential for productive refocalization to address contemporary issues.

The interface between orality and literature, then, is best seen as one continually mediated by ideological and aesthetic factors. And since, as has already been pointed out, the traditional resource base is constantly in a dialogical interaction with different contexts, it is difficult to make the analysis of the relationship between orality and literature solely in terms of the quest for stabilised entities. It seems best to recognise that the field of culture is always in a *process* of self-creation and to proceed from there. If we are going to learn anything from anthropology to apply to literature, it is going to be that the field of orality requires as much careful theorisation as has been accorded that of textuality. And whatever theory it is we apply in analyses is one which must itself foreground new *processes* and *procedures* of investigation located at the meeting place of different disciplines, thus reaping the full connotational charge of the term "symbol" in Ortner's usage to help us grapple with the full complexity of both orality and of literature.

1   In this forthcoming essay Karin Barber explores these ideas and shows how Yorùbá language literature, as an example of non-Europhone writing, has developed its own standards of viability both in terms of the literary models it deploys and the size of audience it addresses.
2   A few notable examples are Beier 1967, Obiechina 1975, and Palmer 1979.
3   Paul Rabinow (1986) notes some of the dangers inherent in an unexamined confidence in the principle of dialogical ethnographies. He points out in a critique of Clifford and Geertz contained in *Writing Culture* that it is often the case in their own writings that an espousal of dialogical motivations is articulated by means of monological ethnographic discourses.

4   Anthony Appiah (1992) takes a different attitude to these discourses. For him they are not ethnic but racialist discourses that are grounded on a misapprehension of the constitution of "race" when it is defined mainly in terms of biological factors. I do not fully agree with his handling of the Pan-Africanist discourses and his analysis of the post-colonial attitude of Third-world intellectuals, but his work is important because, unlike Miller, he perceives these racialist discourses as having incendiary potentials which must be properly theorized in their global implications.

5   It is important to note that Miller is not alone in this homogenising tendency. Something of this tendency towards homogenising the Other can be glimpsed in works as theoretically different as Walter Ong's *Orality and Literacy* and Jameson's "Third-World Literature in the Era of Multinational Capitalism." In Ong's case the problem arises with his perception of the two categories of orality and literacy as unified and stable concepts allowing him to postulate differences in the conceptual abilities of different peoples as being essentially that of the presence or absence of writing. The reification of the category of writing and the subtle implication of its talismanic ability to generate sophisticated mental capacities has been criticised generally by Brian V Street (1984), but no one seems to have tackled Ong directly. Jameson, on the other hand, conducts an uncharacteristically reductionist reading of Third-World literatures to suggest that they can all be read as "national allegories." His gross generalizations have been starkly exposed by Aijaz Ahmad (1987). But what is significant in both these cases is that the studies are undertaken with the express purpose of correcting Western conceptions of themselves in relation to other cultures. Their flaws reveal the general failure of good intentions to redress the persistence of conservative attitudes to other people's cultures.

6   Ruth Finnegan (1970, 1977) seems to be the most articulate advocate of the necessity for focusing on performance in the analysis of oral literature, but in emphasising performance she ignored various questions to do with power and gender relations in the context of performance.

7   Some of the links have already been noted by Chidi Okonkwo in a Paper entitled "African writers and the quest for order in a changing order" presented to the West African Seminar Series of the African Studies Centre, University of Cambridge, 15 May 1992 and also by Kole Omotoso in a review of Okri's latest novel, *Songs of Enchantment*, in *The Guardian*, 23 March 1993.

8   In a particularly stimulating doctoral dissertation, Joe Eboreime (1992) shows how ethnic identities are negotiated with an eye to the acquisition and maintenance of scarce economic resources in the context of two communities in the Nigerian delta area. This study draws attention to the fact that ethnic

identities are continually being re-negotiated to take account of present-day exigencies.

9   There are important questions in relation to Tutuola's practice that cannot be raised here. What, for instance, is the hierarchization of Yorùbá folktales and why is it that Tutuola ignores the trickster tales of Ijapa the Tortoise and instead focuses on the ones to do with spiritual adventures in the bush? Were there particular cultural issues his tales sought to address? Obiechina (1968) addresses some of the possible cultural implications of Tutuola's early work. Though his central focus seems to be on exploring the work mainly as anthropological data, he still offers ways in which the narratives can be related to wider questions of cultural and literary significance.

10 Gerald Moore (1962) and Harold Collins (1969) both devote attention to the cross-cultural patterns that manifest themselves in Tutuola's work and that place them at par with myths of other peoples.

11 Deidre La Pin (1977) devotes attention to a careful analysis of this and other questions in her work on Yorùbá oral literature.

The Other Half of the Story:
Nigerian Women Telling Tales

Ada Adeghe

As a consequence of their roles in society, African women have always been upholders of tradition. In Nigerian and other African societies, it has often been the primary duty of female members to pass down traditional wisdom, cultural mores and value systems to future generations. Gay Wilentz talks about Black women writers looking back through their mothers, and argues that 'Orature, and consequently, literature are part of many women's daily struggle to communicate, converse, and pass on values to their own children and other children, and one another.'[1]

The importance of this role of women in traditional African life cannot be over emphasised. Through the use of folktales, proverbs, riddles and songs, they convey moral lessons to the younger generation. A failure on the part of a child to grasp and adhere to cultural norms is generally considered a failure on the part of his/her mother. There is a saying in Nigeria that when a child does well, he/she is his/her father's child, but a bad child belongs to his/her mother.

Oladele Taiwo, in his book, *Female Novelists of Modern Africa*, argues that this role is entrusted to women in African societies because 'usually the woman is not as tired after the day's work as the man.'[2] This contradicts his earlier argument about how hard the African woman has to work in order to assist her husband provide for the family. I consider this an important point which must not be ignored, as it helps understand the particular pressures Nigerian women face when they decide to write.

One finds then that the history of African women's literature started long before they held any claim to literacy.

It would be wrong however to assume that the role of African women in oral tradition was limited purely to the handing down of traditional wisdom to their children. Women functioned as performers as well. They were renowned story-tellers and composers of family poetry. The Nigerian female writer, Zaynab Alkali, testifies to this fact. 'I come from an artistic family. My mother sings. My maternal grandmother was a composer/singer and my maternal grandfather was a drummer.'[3] Buchi Emecheta too cites the story-tellers she saw whenever she visited her village as a child. 'I liked the power these women commanded as story-tellers. Since then, I thought I would like to be a story-teller myself.'[4]

In Karin Barber's study of the Oriki of Okuku in Western Nigeria, she notes that some women know a great deal not only of their parent's oriki but also those of their husbands and in-laws. 'These women become known within the compound as experts and are called upon to lead the performance on ritual and festive occasions.'[5]

In many ways therefore Nigerian women writers are doing what most African women have always done in traditional societies before the onset of colonialism. Then women were the custodians of African oral literature and good story-tellers were respected, being regarded as valuable members of society. The Kenyan woman writer Asenath Odaga says that 'with the introduction of formal education, the woman's role as custodian of her people's literature and youth's teacher was hijacked by the new order of things.'[6] The South African, Lauretta Ngcobo, whose great-grandmother, she says, was a composer of family poetry, has expressed similar sentiments. 'Unfortunately, this great literary tradition has been steadily subverted with the introduction of the scripted form of literature. The script has tended to divide society into the educated elite and the uneducated mass of the people.'[7]

One must mention though that not all women story-tellers in African societies saw themselves as performers in the real sense of the word. Some were not even aware that the 'pieces' they produced were of literary value. In Karin Barber's study of Oriki, the *Obirin Ile*, or wives of the household did not consider themselves as entertainers, gifted though they were.

One sees echoes of familiar themes running through oral literature and the written literature of Nigerian women writers. One of the most dominant is the ambiguous position of women in traditional African societies. Some African women writers see African culture as a life-giving force on one hand, while being fairly restrictive on the other. African societies are male dominated and while boys receive all the encouragement to attain the highest peak of intellectual achievement, women, on the other hand, are taught the 'virtues' of humility, passivity, and self-effacement.

Their foremothers lamented this injustice in various ways. Lauretta Ngcobo says, 'My grandmother was one of many wives and the least loved. She gave of her burgeoning spirits in compositions to her children ... Her poetry reveals, in achingly beautiful words, the depths of her pain and her desperate loneliness.'[8]

African women have always questioned the traditional cultural expectations for women to be primarily mothers and wives. Women depended, and to a large extent still depend on men for status and respectability, their fate being defined and determined by their relationship with men. Traditional expectations are such that African women are supposed to achieve lasting contentment only when they marry and their needs and aspirations are gladly subsumed to those of their husbands.'

Some African women have found their roles as wives particularly ambivalent. This results from the oppressive nature of some traditional expectations. Oladele Taiwo gives examples of nuptial chants which play a significant role in admonishing brides in Nigeria. Prospective brides are expected to be virgins and only then do they qualify to sing nuptial songs.

Iwo too n'rele oko	You that you are getting married
Ma ma ta a a ro lola	Do not discountenance the hearth
Ma fi ile Oko sere ale	Do not make jest of marriage institution
Obitun o	Bride
Ma se oran ija nile Oko	Do not cause trouble in the husband's house
Ma soro o pa nile oko ati nibikibi	Do not behave in the way that you will be flogged in your husband's house or anywhere.[9]

These traditional expectations of African women are now being radically questioned by Nigerian women writers. They believe that the much vaunted logic of male superiority in African societies is illogical as it oppresses women and only benefits men. It is alright, they say, if some women do not feel they need to marry, and patriarchal rules are not inviolable. Childlessness, too, should not prevent African women from being reasonably happy in themselves, and living their lives to the full.

Bell Hooks rightly notes that 'certainly for black women, our struggle has not been to emerge from silence into speech but to change the nature and direction of our speech, to make a speech that compels listeners, one that is heard.'[10] Gone are the helpless chants of utter resignation at the position of women under patriarchal rule. One sees a change from the earlier writings of Flora Nwapa which show a general discontent with the situation of women in Nigerian society, to her later works like *One is Enough*,[11] or Emecheta's *Joys of Motherhood*[12] and *Double Yoke*,[13] books which seriously challenge conventional sexist notions of woman's role in marriage, insisting on the importance of female self-actualisation. Like their foremothers in the oral tradition, African women writers sometimes draw upon the painful and debilitating elements of their inner feelings and outer lives as a central focus of their writings. They confront their lives through the resolution achieved in their works.

As I mentioned earlier, Nigerian women have always felt the need to pass on traditional wisdom to younger generations. And that includes lessons they have learnt from their experiences as women in an African society. Evident in the literature of Nigerian women is the strong conviction as to the importance of what they have to say and their right to say it.

But even though some aspects of traditional culture limit women's roles, Nigerian women writers still draw strongly from the orature of their African culture in their written literature. To them, it is a recognition of the importance of the collective nature of their experience. Wilentz uses the term 'Oraliterature' to describe 'written creative works which retain elements of the orature that informed them.'[14]

Orature thus informs the language and the structure of most of their works. The rich borrowings from tradition are replete in Flora Nwapa's earlier novels. Zaynab Alkali's *The Stillborn*[15] is another good example. The village women in these novels strive to maintain the moral values of Nigerian society. They comment on the dire consequences of reneging on their positions as upholders of cultural values, while being fully aware that some cultural expectations restrict their freedom as individuals. Ordinary conversations are punctuated by local proverbs. Characters retain traditional speech patterns as they detail traditional wisdom handed down by ancestors.

Nigerian women writers themselves openly acknowledge their indebtedness to their foremothers' orature. Buchi Emecheta says her novel *The Slave Girl*,[16] is her mother's story. Flora Nwapa, too, has said that ideas for *Idu*[17] and *Efuru*[18] came from her mother.

Oral art is communally created, and while a work of fiction is often one writer's own efforts, there *is* the need to create a work that is meaningful to other members of society, women in particular. Representations of everyday conversations interspersed with praises, proverbs, riddles and cautionary tales are distinctive ways Nigerian women writers derive meaning from their oral tradition. They express a strong commitment to reflect their culture, extolling those customs and traditions they see as beneficial, while dissenting from values they find particularly oppressive to women. In this way, they attempt to reform the culture through their literature.

Emmanuel Obiechina in his study of tradition in West African novels asserts; 'The most noticeable difference between novels written by native West Africans and those by non-natives using West African settings is the important position which the representation of oral tradition is given by the first, and its almost complete absence in the second.'[19]

But Eileen Julien, in her study of African novels, cautions against seeing this drawing upon elements of oral tradition in African fiction as 'an essential fact.' She calls it 'accidental.' In other words, it is misleading to assume 'almost invariably that there is something ontologically oral about Africa and that the act of writing is disjunctive and alien for Africans.'[20]

In the process of saying what they feel is their duty to communicate to their readers, Nigerian women writers face pressures, some rather unique to women in African societies. In various personal interviews, the issue of time seems to be the most glaring. Writers in every society are pressed for time, but in the African situation where traditional expectations are such that a woman's prime role is to 'serve' others, the extended family system imposes demands that often verge on the insurmountable. That pressure, coupled with the dire economic climate in Africa means that writing becomes a self-indulgent activity, for there is really very little money to be made from it. Flora Nwapa captures this problem graphically when asked why we do not have more Nigerian women writers. She says; 'A Nigerian woman faces far too many problems in our society today. She goes to the university to get qualified, when she finishes, she gets a job. Then she gets married. Within a short while she starts having children. Then she has to look after her children and her husband and she also has a job to do ... the extended family comes in. She might be expected to send her younger brothers and sisters to school. How does she do all these? The problems are compounded when, in the situation that we find ourselves today, she has to go out and look for essential commodities, things like milk, soap to wash her clothes and bathe herself, all the things you need in the house. If she doesn't do these things, she will face starvation.'[21]

No sane woman goes buying typing paper and ribbons when she needs milk for her children. This is not an exaggeration and things have gotten worse since that interview was given. Under such conditions, the 'need to write' pales into insignificance.

Writing is anyway a rather private and lonely business. Born and bred into large families, it is rather difficult for Nigerian women to remove themselves from it all, withdraw to an isolated place to write. While it is permissible for a man to withdraw into his study to write, it is not always the case for a woman. Buchi Emecheta told me in a personal interview that while she feels the need to travel to Nigeria as often as she can, she could not have written all the books she has written if she settled permanently in Nigeria.

Illiteracy is still widespread in Nigeria, and that poses a major problem for writers and publishers alike. Even educated Nigerians have not cultivated the habit of reading outside set texts for school. Reading for pleasure is not one of our strong points and people just do not feel they need to read fiction. Even the government lacks the appreciation for home produced literary works and does little to encourage writers financially or otherwise.

When the foremothers of Nigerian women writers imparted cultural mores and traditional wisdom, it was done spontaneously. There were the occasional set times for folk tales and moonlit games, but most of the time, it was in the course of carrying out household duties that the process of inculcating cultural mores and values into children took place.

But writing *is* different. You need to take time out. Time out of your maternal duties to sit down and write. And in various interviews, these women have often lamented the difficulties involved in doing just that in the Nigerian situation.

One has to mention too the neglect which African women writers receive from the critical establishment. Such indifference to their writings, they find, extremely demoralising. Even though a lot of their writings are comparable to those of their male counterparts, they do not get the same critical space. This neglect is evident in the oral genres as well. Yet women have traditionally displayed considerable talent in this field. I believe this attitude to African women's writings stems from the overwhelmingly patriarchal arrangement of the critical establishment.

There is more to writing than mere words on a page. To register socially and acquire value and meaning, writers have to be discussed and this involves publishers, critics - activities and institutions beyond the individual writers.

With oral performances, there is instant criticism which the traditional artist finds rewarding and highly beneficial. The performer is not ignored. Everyone knew when a performance was innovative and the performer was praised. A performance devoid of creativity and fresh insight, courted criticism.

> Well a tale is not a tale
> Without a word or two on how it fares:
> My ears are opened to the ground
> For what errors you may find.
> It is simple and plain
> That one hand cannot wash a story clean:
> It needs the help of the other.[22]

The Nigerian woman writer rarely enjoys such objective communal criticism. It is ironical in fact that one area where women are thoroughly despised today in Nigeria is in the field of drama and performance. Many people feel that respectable women should not be performing on stage. But when African women write plays, they expect them to be performed as it is in performance that a play comes alive. Husbands cannot put up with long hours required for producing plays. Men do not even approve of their daughters becoming performers. As to the disrespect with which women performers are now treated, one finds it rather strange as African foremothers were the story-tellers, praise singers and dancers of African villages.

And to think that one of the most idealised images in African literature today, is that of the African woman as the custodian of traditional values.

---

1   Wilentz 1992: xiv.
2   Taiwo 1984: 7.
3   James 1990: 32.
4   Ibid, 37.
5   Barber 1991: 12.
6   Interview in *West Africa*, 26 October - 1 November 1992: p.1848.
7   Ngcobo 1985.

8   Ibid.
9   Taiwo 1984: 8.
10   Hooks 1989.
11   Nwapa 1981.
12   Emecheta 1979.
13   Emecheta 1982.
14   Wilentz 1992: xvii.
15   Alkali 1988.
16   Emecheta 1976.
17   Nwapa 1970.
18   Nwapa 1966.
19   Obiechina 1975.
20   Julien 1992: 8.
21   James 1990: 32.
22   Mapanje and White, p.4.

"Writin in Light": Orality-thru-typography, Kamau Brathwaite's
Sycorax Video Style

Stewart Brown

This essay has evolved from what seemed to me, at least initially, a paradox -
that Kamau Brathwaite should assert that his 'discovery' of the word processor's hi-
tech typographical possibilities was an agent for the development and presentation
as text of the essentially oral 'nation language' of the Caribbean. I raised this issue
with Brathwaite when I interviewed him in Jamaica in 1988, in a discussion about
X/Self, the volume in which his poem 'X/Self's Xth Letters from the Thirteen
Provinces' appears, which included the lines

    (I'm)
    'learnin prospero linguage &

    ting

    not fe dem/ not fe dem
    de way caliban

    done

    but fe we
    fe-a-we

    for not one a we should responsible if prospero get curse
    wid im own

    curser'
    ....

    yet a sittin down here in front a dis stone
    face/eeee

    lectrical mallet into me
    fist

    chipp/in dis poem onta dis tablet
    chiss/ellin darkness writin in light[1]

I had interpreted these passages, playing with the language of the word processor and punning between the codes of his poetic nation language and that hi-tech jargon as drawing attention to a kind of conflict between technology and the history/conditions from which nation language emerged. But no, Brathwaite said,

> "Quite the opposite. What I was saying there was that technology makes nation-language <u>easier</u> ... the 'global village concept, the message is the medium and all that ... The poem was saying that the computer has made it much easier for the illiterate, the Caliban, actually to get himself visible ... Because the computer does it all for you. You don't have to be able to type, you can make mistakes and correct them or leave them, <u>you can see what you hear</u>. When I said "writin in light", that is the main thing about it - the miracle of that electronic screen means that the spoken word can become visible in a way that it cannot become visible in the typewriter where you have to erase physically .... The computer has moved us away from scripture into some other dimension which is "writin in light". It is really nearer to the oral tradition than the typewriter is. The typewriter is an extension of the pen. The computer is getting as close as you can to the spoken word.[2]

I want to explore, briefly, the evidence for that assertion and to look at the ways Brathwaite's early work, both as cultural historian/critic and poet, anticipated that concern with the representation of an oral language as text and with the ways text could be arranged to suggest the enunciation of the language. I would hope, then, to trace the logic of the ways his subsequent work has developed towards such a visually distinctive presentation/experimentation with language, particularly in terms of the 'Sycorax video style' he has evolved through his collections *Middle Passages, DreamStories* and *Barabajan Poems*.

The date of *Middle Passages* publication was significant - 1992 being the 500th anniversary of Columbus's entry into the/his New World. Kamau Brathwaite is an academic historian whose work has focused on the ramifications and distortions engendered by that 'discovery'. His work in various genres, for his historical research has always informed his poetry, indeed the two great trilogies for which he is best known in the literary world - *The Arrivants* and *Mother Poem, Sun Poem* and *X/Self* - represent his engagement with the human effects and issues of that brutal history. His historical imagination, as mediated through his poetry, is informed by his experience of living for many years in Ghana, and, on his return to the Caribbean, by his recognition of the submerged presence of Africa in the cultures of the region. Much of his work has been a kind of reclamation of that African inheritance, a reclamation that has inevitably involved a process of challenge and confrontation with the elements of the mercantilist/colonial culture which overlaid and often literally oppressed the African survivals.

Just as he insisted in his scrupulous - but also controversial - study, *The Development of Creole Society in Jamaica 1770-1820* that the slaves most important act of resistance to the slavers' attempts at domination was through their refusal, adaptation and appropriation of the slavers' language,

'It was in language that the slave was perhaps most successfully imprisoned by his masters; and it was in his (mis-) use of it that he perhaps most effectively rebelled. Within the folk tradition, language was (and is) a creative act in itself; the word was held to contain a secret power ...' [3]

so Brathwaite's most fundamental challenge to the cultural status quo has been to the language of cultural domination itself, and to its most privileged form, as book-bound, grammar-bound script. He has consistently championed the use of non-standard vocabularies, refusing the implicit pejoratives of 'dialect' and even 'creole' as terms to describe the languages that Caribbean people speak, instead coining and asserting the appropriateness of the term 'nation language' to reflect both the status of that spoken tongue and the fact of the differences between the languages of the various nations of the West Indies.

Brathwaite argued, in his *History of the Voice* (1984), for the cultural and psychological importance of nation language at many levels. Evolving from the very history of the places where it is spoken, it enables speech, he argues, where the dominant language cannot cope with the local referents

'...the models are all there for the falling of snow ...(but we haven't got the syllables, the syllabic intelligence, to describe the hurricane, which is our own experience...the hurricane does not roar in pentameters'.[4]

In his lecture 'Caribbean Culture: Two Paradigms' published in 1983 but originating somewhat earlier, Brathwaite described his increasing frustration with the resources of English in his quest to make an authentically Caribbean poetry, true to his experience and feeling,

'In addition to the natural poet's desire to transplode words, I find increasingly, as the struggle to express our particular experience in the general vocabulary of an admittedly generous language, that one has to create words to fit our particular and peculiar experience. It is the crisis of conscious Caliban faced with Prospero's thesaurus'.[5]

Finding a language for that which cannot be said in the 'official' language is clearly potentially subversive of that language's dominance and it is that subversive quality which Brathwaite fundamentally values. Nation-language represents, he argues in *History of the Voice*, the enunciation of "the African aspect of our New World/Caribbean heritage"[6] which must inevitably be at odds with the linguistic and grammatical as well as the cultural and ideological status quo. He argues too that nation-language is an essentially oral/aural medium, its orality another aspect of its challenge to the dominance of a text inflected English.

'[Nation language] exists not in the dictionary but in the tradition of the spoken word. It is based as much on sound as it is on song. That is to say, the noise that it makes is part of its meaning, and if you ignore the noise (or what you would think of as noise shall I say) then you lose part of the meaning. <u>When it is written, you lose the sound of the noise and therefore you lose part of the meaning</u>' [my emphasis].[7]

But this does not mean that Brathwaite would limit a contemporary Caribbean word-culture to its oral dimension alone; as poet, publisher, historian, editor, essayist, critic, bibliographer and archivist he has always been very much engaged with texts, with the printed forms of language, and indeed argues the important place of texts <u>alongside</u> the oral word-culture.[8] What his work more and more reflects is his quest to find ways in which texts can be made to accommodate the 'noise' of nation-language, to represent the "new shapes and consciousness of ourselves"[9] which the use of that language allows. It is interesting to note that even in the early nineteen-eighties, when *History of the Voice* was being constructed, he was beginning to think in terms of the computer in the way he described that quest, speaking of trying to catch "the actual rhythms and syllables, <u>the very software</u>, in a way, of the language."[10] [my emphasis]

There is evidence of this concern right through his work. His use of a range of voices across the continuum of creole registers in *The Arrivants*, privileging the peasant voice in crucial poems like 'The Dust' - which has become now a classic expression of West Indian consciousness - is in part an aspect of Brathwaite's attempt to break and break away from the cultural constraints of English. Brathwaite refers back to 'The Dust' in 'X/Self's Xth Letters from the Thirteen Provinces', the ending of the later poem, with the persona's somewhat frightened, suspicious query about the sense of power this new technology allows him, "*why is/ dat?//what it/ mean?*" echoing the god fearing, awestruck questioning of the peasant woman's voice at the end of 'The Dust', struggling to find a language to confront the unknown. It is an intriguing echo, the poet perhaps inviting his readers to see the connection between the quest for a language and the 'solution' the computer offers..? Interestingly, he omits that ending echo in 'Letter Sycorax', the revised version of 'X/Self's Xth Letters from the Thirteen Provinces', which appears in *Middle Passages*.

Alongside that concern to allow more voices to be head there has been an ever-present concern with orthography, as if the very technology of printing were loaded against the enunciation of the new/old/evolving oral-now-literary languages he wants to use. From his earliest collections Brathwaite has experimented with layouts and with syntactical 'calibanisms' as he calls them - spelling, breaking, spacing, shaping words in ways that dislocate them from their familiar associations and meanings but more importantly allowing nuances, echoes, puns, rhymes and particular kinds of music 'out' of the language that history has imposed on him to express his experience and vision.

Alongside that cultural imperative there are both modernist and formalist dimensions to this linguistic experimentation. Brathwaite has acknowledged the influence of T.S. Eliot and Ezra Pound on his early attitudes to poetry. There was a cultural connection in the sense that both Eliot and Pound were 'colonials' who took on the poetic establishment as it were, rebellious figures who wanted to make a poetry appropriate to their times and circumstances, to, in Pound's famous phrase, make it new, in a language which bore "the taste of men's mouths". As Donald Hall has observed, for them, breaking away from a colonial model, "eccentricity - formal and spiritual - was an escape from Englishness."[11] Eliot's influence is particularly apparent in terms of his experiments with voices - Brathwaite has said that Eliot's major contribution to the development of Caribbean literature was via his validation of "the speaking voice, the conversational tone."[12] Eliot's interest in jazz and his adaptation of some jazz-like techniques, also seems to have had a significant influence on Brathwaite's approach to the structure of his work in terms of freeing up Brathwaite's language and validating the whole process of dislocating the reader from his/her expectations by mixing languages and scripts within the texts of his poems, laying the poem out in unusual ways and using devices like the list or the repetition of phonetic/rhythmic sounds.

Eliot's experimentation was validated by Pound, who had himself learnt from William Morris and what Jerome McGann calls "the late nineteenth century Renaissance of Printing", that "the physical presentation of texts was a fundamental feature of their expressiveness."[13] The resonances of the re-discovery spread wide, including, interestingly, to include some of the most important work of the Harlem Renaissance in the 1920s. McGann remarks that the radical/racial ideas and attitudes embodied in early works by Langston Hughes, Countee Cullen and in Alain Locke's anthology *The New Negro* are reinforced or reflected in the typographical and spacial manipulations of the text, which are recognised as significant "resources for poetic effects."[14] Brathwaite's experiments with the formatting of words on the page as a means of indicating the particular nuances of spoken voices perhaps owes as much to the work of another American poet of that period, Louis Zukofsky, who argued that "if print and the arrangement of it will help tell how the voice should sound"[15] then typography was clearly a legitimate area of concern for the poet.

Although it may seem radical such typographic foregrounding[16] has a long history; in a recent study the linguist Willie Van Peer trades such devices back to Greek Bucolic poetry in the fourth century BC and cites examples through time, right up to the concrete poets of the nineteen seventies and eighties. The reasons why individual poets in the tradition Van Peer identifies have chosen to draw attention to certain aspects of their texts in this way obviously varies but Van Peer's general assertion is that the conventional distinguishing characteristics of poetry - as distinct from prose - as text - i.e. its layout on the page, its use of white space around lines and stanzas, its use of capital letters at the beginning of lines whether or not that word was the beginning of a sentence, etc. in fact derive from poetry's roots in an oral tradition which were "gradually reconstituted ... with a more predominantly *visual* character."[17] One thing that the poets, like Zukofsky, who have deviated from that 'standard' layout and usage of typography have done is indeed to draw attention back to the implicit signalling of orality by the textual 'surface' of the poem-on-the-page and then to have emphasised aspects of that oral presence by their particular breaking of the conventions in terms of the positioning of the text on the page, line endings, word spacing, type size, italicisation, etc.

Certainly that reorienting/re-oraling of the text has been a crucial aspect of Brathwaite's practice, but his motivations have been historical and cultural rather than formalist or purely linguistic. His typographical experimentation has always been linked to his sense of the English language's complicity - perhaps especially the language-as-text's complicity - in the making of that history which so dominates his imagination and his poetry. Indeed one of the things that distinguishes Brathwaite's experiments from the work of the contemporary concrete/sound poets[18] is that for those artists, as Berjouhi Bowler remarks in her book *The Word as Image*, the visual effect is, if not all, it is certainly their paramount concern. Even though they are interested in the idea that

"by disassociating the word from its usual setting, breaking it down to syllables, or even by giving us the merest reminiscence of a word, (they) make us perceive language spoken or written in a way we had not done before...."

- which is certainly part of what Brathwaite's experiments are about - for the concrete poets the new word-image they construct

". . . wants nothing to do with personality, psychology or biography. It is even removed from history."[19]

Brathwaite's experiments with the arrangement of words on the page has been rather to construct a language that enables the expression of personality, psychology and biography, and while he may wish to make a language able to shuck off the cultural baggage of its received history he also very much wants that new language to be able to express his alternative view of history.

Although the calibanisms, the mutations and amputations of the 'standard' language, the unusual line breaks and layouts, etc. were evident in his work from *Rights of Passage* and had been becoming more pronounced as his work progressed, in *Middle Passages* (1992) that typographic foregrounding seems to have reached a new level in terms of the challenge to grammatical and orthographic orthodoxy. A note among the publication and copyright details announces that the "Text is based on the 'Sycorax video style' being developed by Kamau Brathwaite" and the book employs a variety of fonts, caligraphies and symbols, varying in scale from the minuscule to the massive, both within and between poems. The collection re-works and re-contextualises several of Brathwaite's earlier poems - as in a kind of jazz suite - and it is particularly interesting, in terms of the focus of this paper, to compare the version of 'X/Self's Xth Letters from the Thirteen Provinces' that appears in *X/Self* with the one that appears in *Middle Passages* as 'Letter Sycorax'.

In terms of the literary/linguistic 'content' - the actual words of the poem - there is very little change (a few changes in spelling - which I suspect may be corrections of the OUP editors' earlier 'corrections', i.e. 'reminton' in 'Letter Sycorax' for 'remmington' in the earlier version) until near the very end of the piece, where 'Letter Sycorax' expands and opens out the image of the displaced Africans' journey as one "perpetual/plantation" treadmill experience that is stated in the earlier version with a visual/aural enactment in sound of that experience

how

ever you

runnin up runnin up runnin up

it still

goin down

goin down

goin down

goin down

and a catalogue of the names of those responsible for - or symbols of - that seemingly endless decline, like

. . . grandmaster sergeant doe &

brand new imperial corporals smilin of cordite &

leather

(*Middle Passages*, p.86)

And then, as I remarked above, the ending is changed by the omission of the echo back to 'The Dust' to become a more affirmative - if equally problematic in terms of affixing 'meaning' - statement

&

mamma!

But leaving the textual changes and the effect of the ending aside, the main difference between the two versions is in their layout and their use of typographic emphasises like the italicisation of many of the words at the beginning of the poem, the use of bold rather than standard typefaces in certain places and the replacing of the conventional lower case x - and certain words - in the poem by the large and visually intrusive X symbol from another font altogether, as aspects of Brathwaite's Sycorax video style. The effect of those changes are interesting; the major layout change, which does change the whole appearance of the poem on the page, is the shift from a conventional columnar left justification of the text in the OUP *X/Self* version, to the centring of each line in 'Letter Sycorax' which, somehow, becomes much easier to actually read, perhaps because the layout no longer asks us to read the text as conventional English poem, with all the unconscious but powerful associations/expectations of line endings, rhythmic patterns and patterns of narrative that the recognition of that basic shape-on-the-page imposes on our reading. Laid out as it is in the latter version, the poem visually rejects those conventions, it no longer signals as the broken couplets of an English poem but signals that this text will ask something else of its reader. In effect the Sycorax video style frees both the text and the reader from those 'interference' effects that carry over from those cultural expectations triggered by the essentially traditional format of the original version and allow the rhythmic patterns and linguistic effects to make their own music - we do not unconsciously read this text against our expectations of the ways poems conventionally work. In his provocative book *Poetry as Discourse* the critic Anthony Easthope is at pains to establish the significance of such expectations, arguing that poetic forms are never ideologically neutral but signify particular, historic associations and allegiances on the part of the user which the reader will almost invariably pick up.[20] By arranging his text in the way he does in 'Letter Sycorax' Brathwaite is retaining the distinction between poetry and prose that the conventional poetic layout claims but distancing his text from the cultural associations of that layout.

Laid out under the Sycorax video style the poem is visually much more distinctive that in the earlier version and recalls Brathwaite's remark that what he is trying to do with these new layouts is create "word sculpture on the page, word sculpture in the ear"[21], creations which inevitably require a different set of aesthetic criteria for their appreciation than would be applied to traditional poems. But more significantly, as that remark makes clear, the layouts also serve to direct would-be reader/speakers of the poems into an understanding of the ways he intends the music of the poems to move, to be heard. As he said in the interview referred to earlier, the layout of the poems is "part of my own concept of how they should sound and a hopeful aid to another reader." For Brathwaite's poems - while they repay careful scrutiny as texts - do live in their enunciation. To know a Brathwaite poem only from its text on the page and then to see/hear him read it is to understand how much of his work relies on the power of the spoken word. Brathwaite himself regards this as a very important aspect of his work; asked about the importance of performance in that same interview, he remarked

"I think there is always a little confusion about my work in that I <u>don't</u> perform at all, its my poetry that does it, I hardly move my body. And I think that the critics ought to begin to look at that because it's something that I think is my major contribution, if any, to the whole development of our poetry, (is) that the words on the page have a metaphorical life of their own. I do not depend upon walking up and down on the stage and doing things. People have the impression that I'm performing when in fact they are actually dealing with poetry as they ought to, that is, the poetry is singing in their ears."

Understanding then that performance, in relation to Brathwaite's work, means enunciation, there is a sense in which the texts of his poems are 'scripts for performance.' That is a phrase which has some resonance in the discussion of Caribbean poetry - a phrase which Louise Bennett, or at least her critical champions, objected to when it was applied to her work by some well meaning TLS reviewer, because it seemed to limit her to an oral arena and deny her poetry the status accorded to 'real' literature. In Brathwaite's case however, given his statements above, it is perhaps possible to read such a judgement as a <u>liberation</u> of the poem from the limitations of the conventions of text-bound 'literature'. So the world turns!

Brathwaite has used versions of the Sycorax video format in the three other books that have appeared since *Middle Passages*; *The Zea-Mexican Diary*[22], *Barabajan Poems*[23] and *DreamStories*[24]. Although *The Zea-Mexican Diary* employs a larger than conventional typeface and makes use of some of the strategies for emphasis that the other texts employ in order to stress particular emotional changes in the lamentation/celebration that is the substance of the diary, it is essentially a conventional prose narrative and the typographical effects are minimised[25]. The *DreamStories* couldn't be more unconventional either intrinsically, as narratives, or in the ways that they are laid out on the page in the Longman edition. As Gordon Rohlehr observes in his introduction to the collection, the devices of the Sycorax video style

create an arbitrariness in the appearance of the text,
corresponding to the arbitrariness of the different dream
worlds of these stories.[26]

The text is full of calibanisms and perverse punctuation marks which jar and disrupt the conventional flow of the narrative and Brathwaite employs all the devices of emphasis mentioned above, particularly in terms of varying the scale of the letter forms within and between words and being aware of the white space of the page to create the DreamStory effect. Part of that effect is to blur the divide between the visual-verbal language of dream as it is experienced and the capture/re-creation of that experience <u>as text</u> that might assist the re-enactment of the experience by the 'reader' as sound and (in)sight. The analogy seems to me to be with a musical score, particularly the scores of some contemporary composers who are trying to break new musical ground, in that the score is made of symbols that can be read and coded instructions that can be followed, so that practised readers can 'play' the music in their heads from the printed score, but the music only really fulfils its potential/ becomes itself in its performance. Similarly the Sycorax video texts demand enunciation or at least a kind of active engagement on the part of the reader beyond the 'naturalised' process of silent reading or study. In a note to the story 'Dream Chad' Brathwaite refers to the story as it is written in light, in the word processor, as "oratory".[27] The music analogy is perhaps better expressed, knowing Brathwaite's own taste in music and the experiments he has done throughout his career with jazz, if we think of the Sycorax video style as the *enjazzment* of the literary process, so that these stories become jazz texts.

The *DreamStories* text, as it appears in the Longman edition, while it may give the illusion of 'arbitrariness' is in fact far from arbitrary and - although it did not end up quite as Brathwaite originally envisaged it - much wrangling and hand-wringing was involved in the production of the book even to get it as close as it is in this edition to his original idea. Indeed the author spent an entire summer re-formatting the text, as the best version the publisher could make - by reducing the scale of Brathwaite's original typescript to match the format of the series in which the book appears - did not meet Brathwaite's requirements in terms of the text's appearance and the aesthetic effects it generated.[28]

Given that Brathwaite could effectively act as publisher as well as author of the text, *Barabajan Poems*, published by Savacou North in 1994, represents the first opportunity to fully utilise the Sycorax video style format. The book is a mammoth tome, over 400 A4 pages, and utilises all the graphic potential of the word-processor's manipulation of printed language. The book is an expanded version of the 12th Sir Winston Scott Memorial lecture given in Barbados in 1987. It is, in effect, a kind of autobiography, a reprise of the ways in which Brathwaite's poetry has engaged with Barbados, its landscape, history and people over the course of his career explaining his relationship to earlier writers and his view of the potential for a flowering of Bajan consciousness in literature. The text is laid out and shaped according to the particular effects Brathwaite is trying to achieve, from a more or less conventional prose layout for the passages that stay close to the text of the lecture, through the by now characteristic calibanisms and use of different typefaces interspersed with graphic devices like arrows, boxes and clip-art pictograms within the texture of the piece, through to whole pages of poems in which the text is centred and very large pitch letter forms are used - so that on several pages there are only a dozen or so words. One purpose of the large type texts, centred in a field of white paper is to lend a particular importance to the words thus emphasised and one whole section of the book in which that technique is used is devoted to Bajan proverbs and "small-ilann saying(s)" like

sea

doan have no
BACKDOOR

(Barabajan Poems p.282)

Common speech, everyday language, ordinary usage here made extraordinary by the manner of its presentation as text. The Sycorax layouts also develop on the effect observed in 'Letter Sycorax', above, of easing, directing and enabling the transition from text to speech and generally challenging the readerly presumptions inscribed into traditional/conventional texts, but the *Barabajan Poems* project is essentially an academic intervention and the overall shape of that academic discourse places some limits on the appropriate application of the Sycorax video style.

So we must wait for the appearance of a new book of new poems/stories, composed and conceived in the new format rather than translated up into it as most of the poems in *Middle Passages* and *Barabajan Poems* were, and which is also designed/published according to Brathwaite's specifications rather than reduced by the conventions/demands of a publishing house as *DreamStories* was, before we can fully measure the impact of the Sycorax video style. But if we accept that the Caribbean isles are indeed "full of noises" which formal, traditional English-as-text cannot adequately represent, it is clear that in the process of resisting the conventional pressures of the text in order to give voice to the noise of nation language on the page, Brathwaite's writin-in-light Sycorax video style is both a logical development of his own creative practice and another step on the road Caribbean poets have been treading - arguably since Francis Williams but certainly since Claude McKay - towards finding a means of accommodating the language of life as it is sounded in the Caribbean and the life of letters as they are printed on the page.

---

1 Brathwaite, 1987: 84/5, 87.
2 The full text of the interview is published in *Kyk-over-al* (Georgetown, Guyana) No.40, 1989 : 84-93.
3 Brathwaite 1970: 17.
4 Brathwaite 1984: 8, 10.
5 Brathwaite 1983: 9-54.
6 Brathwaite 1984: 13.
7 Ibid: 17.
8 Ibid: 49. "To confine our definitions of literature to written texts in a culture that remains ital in most of its people proceedings is as limiting as its opposite:

135

trying to define Caribbean literature as essentially orature - like eating avacado without its likkle salt."

9 Ibid: 49.

10 Ibid: 8.

11 Hall 1969: 12.

12 Brathwaite, 1984: 30.

13 McGann, 1993: 77.

14 McGann, 1993: 81.

15 Zukofsky, Louis, ed. The "Objectivist" Anthology, 1932 p.83, cited in McGann, 1993: 83.

16 I have borrowed the term and much of the substance of the comments in this paragraph from an article by Willie van Peer, 'Typographic foregrounding', in Language and Literature, vol.2, No. 1, 1993: 49-59.

17 van Peer, Ibid., 51.

18 There are some grounds for comparison with more literary figures like Ian Hamilton Finlay whose appreciation of the effects of space around 'poetic' statements come to mind when one looks at some of the passages of Barabajan Poems.

19 Bowler, p.14.

20 Easthope 1976:65.

21 Quoted on the back cover of DreamStories.

22 Brathwaite 1993.

23 Brathwaite 1994.

24 Brathwaite 1994.

25 Anne Walmsley argues, rather, in her essay 'Her Stem Singing: Kamau Brathwaite's Zea-Mexican Diary', (in World Literature Today, vol.68, no.4, Autumn 1994, p.747-749) that The Zea-Mexican Diary represents a particularly subtle and appropriate use of the Sycorax video style.

26 Brathwaite 1994, p.viii.

27 Ibid, p.47-50.

28 Personal discussion with both the poet and the Longman publisher Rosalind Ward.

BIBLIOGRAPHY

Adépojù, Olánrewájú, 1972, *S'àgbà di wèrè*. Ìbàdàn: Oníbonòjé Press.

Ahmad, Aijaz, 1987, "Jameson's Rhetoric of Otherness and the "National Allegory." *Social Text* 17: 3-25.

Alkali, Zaynab, 1988, *The Stillborn*. Essex: Longman.

Appiah, Kwame Anthony, 1992, *In My Father's House: Africa in the Philosophy of Culture*. London: Methuen.

Ashcroft, Bill, Gareth Griffiths and Helen Tiffin, 1989, *The Empire Writes Back: theory and practice in post-colonial literatures*. London: Routledge.

Barber, Karin, 1987, "Popular Arts in Africa", *African Studies Review*, 30, 3.

Barber, Karin, 1991, *I Could Speak Until Tomorrow: Oriki, Women and the Past in a Yorùbá Town*. Edinburgh: Edinburgh University Press.

Barber, Karin, 1991, "Multiple Discourses in Yorùbá Oral Literature." *Bulletin of the John Rylands University Library of Manchester* 73.3 (Autumn): 11-24.

Barber, Karin, "African-Language Literature and Post-Colonial Criticism." To be published in *Imagining Commonwealths*, Ed. T.J.L. Cribb. Cambridge: Cambridge University Press.

Bascom, Harold, 1986, *Apata*. London: Heinemann.

Beier, Ulli, 1967, *Introduction to African Literature*. Evanston: Northwestern University Press.

Bennett, Louise, 1968, interviewed by Dennis Scott in "Bennett on Bennett". *Caribbean Quarterly* 14. 1-2: 98.

Bennett, Louise, 1983, *Yes M'Dear - Miss Lou Live*. Island Records ICT9740.

Bennett, Louise, 1986, 'Back to Africa' in P. Burnett, (ed.) *The Penguin Book of Caribbean Verse in English*. Harmondsworth: Penguin.

Bennett, Louise, 1988, *Jamaica Labrish*. Jamaica: Sangster's Book Stores.

Berry, Sara S., 1985 *Fathers Work For Their Sons*. University of California Press.

Best, E.C., 1993, *'Banja' excavating, inter-facing and replacing African-Caribbean art. Theory, practice and dynamics of the oral/music/performance/text*. PhD thesis, Centre of West African Studies, University of Birmingham.

Bjorkman, Ingrid 1989, *Mother Sing for Me: People's Theatre in Kenya*. London: Zed Books.

Boal, Augustus, 1979, *Theatre of the Oppressed* trans. Charles A & Maria-Odiba Leal McBride. London: Pluto.

Bowler, Berjouhi Barsamian, *The Word as Image*. London: Studio Vista.

Boyarin, Jonathan, (ed.) 1993 *The Ethnography of Reading*. Berkeley: University of California Press.

Brathwaite, E.K., 1970, *Folk Culture of the Slaves in Jamaica*. London: New Beacon Books.

Brathwaite, E.K., 1983, 'Caribbean Culture: Two Paradigms', in Jurgen Martini, (ed.) *Missile and Capsule*. Bremen: University of Bremen.

Brathwaite, E.K., 1984, *History of the Voice*. London: New Beacon Books.

Brathwaite, E.K., 1987, *X/Self*. Oxford: OUP.

Brathwaite, Kamau, 1993, *The Zea Mexican Diary: 7 Sept.1926 - 7 Sept. 1986*. Madison: University of Wisconsin Press.

Brathwaite, Kamau, 1994, *Barabajan Poems*. New York: Savacou North.

Brathwaite, Kamau, 1994, *DreamStories*. Harlow: Longman.

Brown, Stewart, 1991, *The Art of Derek Walcott*. Bridgend: Seren Books.

Brown, Stewart and Ian McDonald, (eds.) 1992, *The Heinemann Book of Caribbean Poetry*. London: Heinemann.

Brown, Stewart, Mervyn Morris and Gordon Rohlehr, 1989, (eds.) *Voiceprint*. Harlow: Longman.

Brutus, Dennis, 1973, 'Postscripts' in *Collected Poems of South African Jail and Exile*. London: Heinemann.

Burnett, P., 1986, (ed.) *The Penguin Book of Caribbean Verse in English*. Harmonsworth: Penguin.

Cagnolo, C., 1933, *The Akikuyu: Their Customs, Traditions and Folklore*. Nyeri: Kenya: The Mission Printing School.

Cagnolo, C., 1952-53, Vol. 12, Kikuyu Tales, *African Studies*.

Cassidy, F. & R. B. Le Page, 1967, 1980, *Dictionary of Jamaican English*. Cambridge: Cambridge University Press.

Cassidy, F., 1961, *Jamaica Talk: Three Hundred Years of the English Language in Jamaica*. London: Macmillan.

Chukwuma, 'The Oral Tale' in Peterson, J.H. & Rutherford, A., eds., 1981, *Cowries & Kobos* (p.12-17).

Clifford, James and George E. Marcus, 1986, *Writing Culture: The Poetics and Politics of Ethnography*. Berkerly: University of California Press.

Collins, Harold R., 1969, *Amos Tutuola*. New York: Twayne.

Cookey, Sylvannus, 1974, *King Ja Ja of The Niger Delta*. New York: NOK.

Cooper, C., "Slackness Hiding From Culture: Erotic Play in the Dancehall" *Jamaica Journal* 22.4 (1989) : 12-20; 23.1 (1990) : 44-51.

Cooper, C., 1989, *Slackness hiding from culture: DJ rule*, Paper presented to the 13th Annual Conference of the Society for Caribbean Studies, Hoddesdon, Herts, U.K.

Cooper, C., "Cho! Missa Cargill, Riispek Juu!" *Sunday Gleaner*, November 5, 1989, 9.

Cooper, Carolyn 1993, *Noises in the Blood: Orality, Gender and the 'Vulgar' Body of Jamaican Popular Culture*. London: Macmillan-Warwick University Caribbean Studies.

D'Costa J. and B. Lalla, (eds.) 1989, *Voices in Exile: Jamaican Texts of the 18th and 19th Centuries*. Tuscaloosa: University of Alabama Press.

De la Mare, Walter, 1918, 'Betrayal' in *Collected Poems*. London: Faber and Faber.

DeLisser, H., 1914, 1981, *Jane's Career*, London: Heinemann.

Easthope, Anthony, 1976, *Poetry as Discourse*. London: Methuen.

Eboreime, Joseph O., 1992, "Group Identities and the Changing Patterns of Alliances Among the Epie-Attissa People of Nigeria, 1890-91." Diss., University of Cambridge.

Egudu, R. and Nwoga, D., 1971, *Igbo Traditional Verse*. London: Heinemann.

Eliot, T.S., 1942, 'The music of poetry' in *On Poetry And Poets*. London: Faber and Faber.

Eliot, T.S., 1963, *Collected Poems*. London: Faber.

Emecheta, Buchi, 1982, *Double Yoke*, London: Ogwugwu Afor.

Emecheta, Buchi, 1979, *The Joys of Motherhood*. London: Allison & Busby Ltd.

Emecheta, Buchi, 1976, *The Slave Girl*. London: Allison & Busby.

Enos, R.L., 1990, 'Sophistic formulae and the emergence of the Attic - Ionic grapholect: a study in oral and written composition', in Enos, R.L. (ed.) *Oral and written communication: historical approaches*. Written Communication Annual, Vol.4. London: Sage.

Ensowanne, Uzo, 1990. 'The Madness of Africa(ns): Or, Anthropology's Reason." *Cultural Critique* 17: 107-26.

Fafunwa, 1974, *History of Education in Nigeria*. Ibadan: NPS Educational.

Fapohunda, O.J., 1985 *The Informal Sector of Lagos: an Inquiry Into Urban Poverty and Employment*. Ibadan: University Press Limited.

Figueroa, J.J., 1970, (ed.), 'Caribbean Voices: an anthology of West Indian poetry, selected by John Figueroa', Volume 2 *The Blue Horizons*. London: Evans Brothers.

Figueroa, J.J., 1982, (ed.), *An anthology of African and Caribbean Writing in English*. London: Heinemann.

Figueroa, J.J., 1989, *Creole in literature: beyond verisimilitude: texture and registers: Derek Walcott*. Paper presented to the 13th Annual Conference of the Society for Caribbean Studies, Hoddesdon, Herts.

Finnegan, Ruth, 1970, *Oral Literature in Africa*. London: Oxford University Press.

Finnegan, Ruth, 1977, *Oral Poetry: Its nature, significance and social context*. Cambridge: Cambridge University Press.

Finnegan, Ruth, 1992, *Oral Traditions and The Verbal Arts*. London: Routledge.

Foucault, Michel, 1977, *Language, counter-memory, practice: selected essays and interviews* (translated D.F. Bouchard & S. Simon), Oxford: Basil Blackwell.

Gilkes, Michael, 1974, *Couvade*, London: Longman.

Gilkes, Michael, 1990, *Couvade*, Mundlestrup, Denmark: Dangaroo.

Gloudon, Barbara, 1982, 'Twenty Years of Theatre', *Jamaica Journal*, No.46.

Gutkind, P.C.W., 1975 "The View From Below: Political Consciousness of the Urban Poor in Ibadan", *Cahiers d'Études Africaines* 15, 1.

Hall, D., 1969, *American Poetry*, London: Faber and Faber.

Harris, Wilson, 1981, "Carnival of Pysche", *Explorations*. Denmark: Dangaroo Press.

Hill, Errol, 1972, *The Trinidad Carnival*. Austin: University of Texas.

Hofmeyr, Isabel, 1994, *We Spend Our Years As A Tale That Is Told: Oral Historical Narrative In A South African Chiefdom*. Johannesburg: Witwatersrand University Press/London: James Currey.

Hooks, Bell, 1989, in *Talking Back: Thinking Feminist - Thinking Black*, . Boston:Gloria Watkins, London: South End Press.

Hountondji, Paulin J., 1983, *African Philosophy: Myth and Reality*. Trans. Henri Evans and Jonathan Rée. Intro. Abiola Irele. Bloomington: Indiana University Press.

Hughes, Langston, 1959, 'Porter' in *Selected Poems*. London: Pluto Press.

Irele, Abiola, 1990, "The African Imagination", *Research in African Literatures*, 21,1.

Jackson, Thomas H., 1991, "Orality, Orature and Ngugi wa Thiong'o' ", *Research in African Literatures*. (Vol.22 No. 1, 5-15).

James, Adeola, 1990, (ed.), *In Their Own Voices: African Women Writers Talk*. London: James Currey.

Jameson, Frederic, 1986, "Third-World Literature in the Era of Multinational Capitalism." *Social Text* 15: 65-88.

Jeyifo, Biodun, 1984, *The Yorùbá Popular Travelling Theatre of Nigeria*. Lagos: Nigeria Magazine Publications.

Julien, Eileen, 1992, *African Novels and the Question of Orality*. Bloomington: Indiana University Press.

Keens-Douglas, P., 1984, 'Communication and the Arts'. Text of an address to the Caribbean Conference of Churches, published in *Caribbean Contact*, October 1984.

La Pin, Deirdre, 1977. "Story, Medium and Masque: the Idea and Art of Yorùbá Storytelling." Diss., University of Wisconsin, Madison.

Larkin, Philip, 1974, 'This Be The Verse', *High Windows*, London: Faber and Faber.

Law, R.C.C., 1973, "The Heritage of Oduduwa: Traditional History and Political Propaganda among the Yorùbá." *Journal of African History* 14.2: 207-22.

Lawuyi, O.B., 1988, "The World of the Yorùbá Taxi-Driver", *Africa* 58, 1.

Lindfors, Bernth, 1980, *Critical Perspectives on Amos Tutuola*. 1975; London: Heinemann.

Long, E., 1774, 1970, *The History of Jamaica*, London: Frank Cass.

Mapanje, J. and White, L., 1983, *Oral Poetry from Africa: an anthology*. Harlow: Longman.

Marshall, Trevor, 1981, *Folk Songs of Barbados*. Bridgetown: MacMarson Associates.

Martin, Toni, 1983, *The PanAfrican Connection*. Dover: Majority Press.

Masilela, Ntongela, 1979, "Ngugi wa Thiong'o's *Petals of Blood*", *Ufahamu: Journal of the African Activist Association*, IX, 2: 20-31.

McGann, Jerome, 1993, *Black Riders: The Visible Language of Modernism*. Princeton, New Jersey: Princeton University Press.

Miller, Christopher L., 1990, *Theories of Africans: Francophone Literature and Anthropology in Africa*. Chicago and London: University of Chicago Press.

Moore, Gerald, 1962, *Seven African Writers*. London: Oxford University Press.

Morris, M., 1989, Printing the performance: 'them' and 'us'. Paper presented to the 13th Annual Conference of the German-speaking countries on the New Literature in English. Giessen, Germany.

Morris, M., 1990, "Printing the Performance", *Jamaica Journal*, 23.1: 21-26.

Ngcobo, Lauretta, 1985, 'My life and my writing' in *Kunapipi*, VIII, 2 & 3 (84).

Njururi, Ngumbi, 1966, *Agikuku Folktales*. London: Oxford University Press.

Nwapa, Flora, 1966, *Efuru*. London: Heinemann.

Nwapa, Flora, 1970, *Idu*. London: Heinemann.

Nwapa, Flora, 1981, *One is Enough*. Enugu: Tana Press Ltd.

Obiechina, Emmanuel N., 1968, "Amos Tutuola and the Oral Tradition." *Présence Africaine* 65: 85-106. Reprinted in Lindfors 84-105.

Obiechina, Emmanuel, 1975, *Culture, Tradition and Society in the West African Novel*. Cambridge: Cambridge University Press.

Ong, Walter J., 1982, *Orality and Literacy: The Technologizing of the Word*. London: Methuen.

Ong, W.J., 1990, 'Technological development and writer - subject - reader immediacies' in Enos, R.L. (ed.) *Oral and written communication: historical approaches*. Written Communication Annual, Vol. 4. London: Sage.

Ortner, Sherry B., 1984, "Theory in Anthropology since the Sixties." *Comparative Studies in Society and History* 26.1: 126-66.

Palmer, Eustace, 1979, *The Growth of the African Novel*. London: Heinemann.

Peel, J.D.Y., 1968, *Aladura: a Religious Movement Among the Yorùbá*. Oxford University Press for the I.A.I.

Peel, J.D.Y., 1978, "Olaju: A Yorùbá Concept of Development", *Journal of Development Studies* 14, 2.

Peel, J.D.Y., 1983, *Ijeshas and Nigerians: the incorporation of a Yorùbá kingdom 1890s - 1970s*. Cambridge: Cambridge University Press.

Peterson, J.H. and Rutherford, A., (eds.), 1981, *Cowries and kobos: the West African oral tale and short story*. Mundelstrup: Dungaroo Press.

Pilgrim, Frank, 1963, *Miriamy*. Georgetown: B.G.Lithographic.

Pilgrim, Frank, 1954, *Skeleton at the Party: a play in one act*. London:Dean and Sons.

Rabinow, Paul, 1986, 'Representations Are Social Facts: Modernity and Post-Modernity in Anthropology.' Clifford and Marcus, 1986, op.cit., 234-261.

Ramchand, K., 1971, *An Introduction to West Indian Literature*. Middlesex: Nelson Caribbean.

Renfrew, C., 1987, *Archaeology and Language The Puzzle of Indo-European Languages*, London: Penguin Books.

Rohlehr, G., 1971, 'West Indian Poetry: Some Problems of Assessment', *Caribbean Quarterly*. Vol.17, nos. 3 & 4 (Sept-Dec.): 92-113.

Rohlehr, G., 1992, *The Shape of that Hurt and other essays*. Port-of-Spain: Longman.

Rohlehr, G., 1992, *My Strangled City and other essays*. Port-of-Spain: Longman.

Rohlehr, G., 1992, *Calypso and Society in Pre-Independence Trinidad*. Port-of-Spain: Gordon Rohlehr.

Sander, Reinhard and Munro, Ian, 1984, "Tolstoy in Africa: an Interview with Ngugi wa Thiong'o' " in G.D. Killam, (ed.) 1984, *Critical Perspectives on Ngugi wa Thiong'o'*. Washington: Three Continents Press.

Sicherman, Carol, 1990, *Ngugi wa Thiong'o' The Making of a Rebel: A Source Book in Kenyan Literature and Resistance*. London: Hans Zell.

Street, Brian V., 1984, *Literacy in Theory and Practice*. Cambridge: Cambridge University Press.

Street, Brian, 1993, (ed.) *Cross-cultural Approaches To Literacy*. Cambridge: Cambridge University Press.

Taiwo, Oladele, 1984, *Female Novelists of Modern Africa*. London: Macmillan.

Thiong'o', Ngugi wa, 1965, *The River Between*. London: Heinemann.

Thiong'o', Ngugi wa, 1977, *Petals of Blood*. London: Heinemann.

Thiong'o', Ngugi wa, 1982, *Devil on the Cross*. London: Heinemann.

Thiong'o', Ngugi wa, 1982, *I Will Marry When I Want*. London: Heinemann.

Turner, Victor, 1969, *The Ritual Process: Structure and Anti-Structure*. London: Routledge and Kegan Paul.

Valery, Paul, 1927, 'Fragment from an inaugural address before the French Academy' (translated Louise Varese), in *Selected Writings of Paul Valery*. New York: New Directions Books.

Valery, Paul, 1950, 'Literature' (translated Louise Varese) in *Selected Writings of Paul Valery*, New York: New Directions Books.

Van Gennep, Arnold, 1960, *The Rites of Passage*. Trans. Monika B. Vizedom and Gabrielle L. Caffee, 1908; London: Routledge and Kegan Paul.

Walcott, Derek 1970, "What the Twilight Says: An Overture", *Dream on Monkey Mountain and Other Plays*. New York: Farrar, Strauss and Giroux.

Walcott, Derek 1973, *Another Life*. London: Jonathan Cape.

Walcott, Derek, 1974, "The Caribbean Culture Or Mimicry", *Journal of Interamerican Studies*, XVL, Feb.1974, 3-13.

Walcott, Derek, 1980, *Remembrance and Pantomime*. New York: Farrar, Strauss and Giroux.

Walmsley, Anne, 1994, 'Her Stem Singing: Kamau Brathwaite's *Zea-Mexican Diary*', *World Literature Today*, 68: 4: Autumn 1994, 747-749.

Warner-Lewis, Maureen 1991, *Guinea's Other Sons*. Dover: The Majority Press.

Waterman, Christopher A., 1990 *Jùjú: a Social History and Ethnography of an African Popular Music*. Chicago University Press.

Wilentz, Gay, 1992, *Binding Cultures: Black Women Writers in Africa and the Diaspora*. Bloomington and Indianapolis: Indiana University Press.

NOTES ON CONTRIBUTORS

Ada Adeghe has recently completed an M.Phil. degree at the Centre of West African Studies, University of Birmingham, on Nigerian Women's Literature. She is also a creative writer on her own account as well as a part-time lecturer in African studies at Winson Green Prison.

Kabir Ahmed is Senior Lecturer and Head of the Department of English and European Languages and Literatures at Usman Danfodio University, Sokoto, Nigeria. In 1992/3 he was a British Council Commonwealth Research Fellow at the Centre of West African Studies. His research interests are in African and Caribbean literatures in English and he has published widely in that field. He is editor of the journal *JELAL*.

Karin Barber is a Senior Lecturer in the Centre of West African Studies. Her teaching and research interests include Yorùbá language, Yorùbá oral literature and culture, African popular culture and African film. She has published many books and essays in those fields, including *I Could Speak Until Tomorrow: Oriki, Women and the Past in a Yorùbá Town*. (Edinburgh, Edinburgh University Press for the International African Institute, 1991).

Curwen Best recently completed his PhD on the analysis of Barbadian popular culture at the Centre of West African Studies. He is presently lecturer in the Department of English at the University of the West Indies in Barbados.

Stewart Brown is a lecturer in the Centre of West African Studies. His research interests are in African and Caribbean literatures in English. He has published several books and essays in those fields, including, as editor, *The Art of Kamau Brathwaite* (Bridgend, Seren Books, 1995).

Al Creighton is Senior Lecturer in the Department of English at the University of Guyana. He has published many essays on aspects of Caribbean literature and is particularly involved in work on West Indian drama. He is well known as a print journalist in Guyana and also produces and presents arts programmes on TV and radio. He is also a poet, a selection of his work is included in the recent anthology *Caribbean New Voices* (Harlow, Longman, 1995).

Carolyn Cooper is Senior Lecturer in the Departments of English/Womens Studies at the University of the West Indies in Jamaica. She was a British Council Commonwealth Research Fellow based at the Centre of West African Studies in

1989/90. Her research interests are in Caribbean popular culture and women's literature. She has published widely in those fields and in 1993 published *Noises in the Blood: Orality, Gender and the 'Vulgar' Body of Jamaican Popular Culture* (Basingstoke, Warwick/Macmillan) which has, like most other things she does, caused a stir!

Hubert Devonish lectures in linguistics at the University of the West Indies in Jamaica. His major publications include *Language and Liberation* (London, Karia Press, 1986.) He is also an accomplished playwright.

Philip Nanton lectures in the Institute of Local Government at the University of Birmingham and is an Honorary Associate Fellow of the Centre of West African Studies. His literary publications include editing the pan-Caribbean anthology *Melanthika* (Birmingham, LWM Publications, 1975), and a selection of his own poems appeared in *The Heinemann Book of Caribbean Verse* (Oxford, 1993).

Femi Oyebode is a psychiatrist by profession, who works at the University/Queen Elizabeth hospital in Birmingham. His literary publications include four much admired collections of poetry, including *Adagio for Oblong Mirrors* (Birmingham, Ijala Press, 1993). He is an Honorary Associate Fellow of the Centre of West African Studies.

Ato Quayson recently completed his PhD at the University of Cambridge on the conceptual links between the writings of Rev. Samuel Johnson, Amos Tutuola, Wole Soyinka and Ben Okri. He is now a Junior Research Fellow at Wolfson College, University of Oxford. His current research interests being African theatre and film and the effect of video technology on the representations of indigenous theatre traditions in Nigeria, Ghana, Zimbabwe and South Africa. He is also Series Editor for the Harwood Press Theatre of African Cultures Series.

Nana Wilson-Tagoe is Professor of African and Caribbean Literature at Kenyatta University, Nairobi in Kenya. In 1992 she was Cadbury Visiting Fellow at CWAS. She has published many books and essays on aspects of African and Caribbean writing, and her major study of West Indian literature is currently in press with Warwick/Macmillan and due for publication in 1995.